Lars Jonsson's Birds

LARS JONSSON'S BIRDS

Paintings from a Near Horizon

Christopher Helm · London

Published in the United Kingdom by Christopher Helm,
an imprint of A&C Black Publishers Ltd.,
36 Soho Square, London W1D 3QY

www.acblack.com

ISBN 978-14081-1014-0

A CIP catalogue record for this book is available from the British Library

This book has been produced by Lars Jonsson.
It is based on the catalogue "Where Heaven and Earth Touch"
which was edited by Peter A. Reimers and Mamoun Fansa and
published in conjunction with the first exhibition of Lars Jonsson's
work in the Federal Republic of Germany in July 2008.
Financial assistance for the printing of the original catalogue
were given by the State of Lower Saxony, the "Landessparkasse"
in Oldenburg, the Cultural Foundation of the "Öffentliche
Versicherung", the "EWE" Foundation and Gertrud and Hellmut
Barthel Foundation, Papier- und Kartonfabrik Varel.

Layout and cover design: Lars Jonsson
Graphic design: Lars Jonsson and Christer Jonson

Translations: Linda Schenk and Erik Hirschfeld

Printed by Fälth & Hässler, Värnamo in October 2008
on Lessebo Linné, yellowtoned 150 gram
and Galerie Art Silk 170 gram.

10 9 8 7 6 5 4 3 2 1

Foreword 7
LARS JONSSON

Lars Jonsson: The Beauty of Nature 17
ADAM DUNCAN HARRIS

About Lars Jonsson 21
KENT ULLBERG

On the Subject of Beauty 23
FREDRIK SJÖBERG

Early works 33

Sketchbooks 45

Watercolours 67

Oilpaintings 123

Ornithological projects 155

Lithographs 177

CHRONOLOGY 183
EXHIBITIONS 187
BIBLIOGRAPHY 191

The distance to the place where the sea is delineated against the sky as a line is, as we see it through our eyes, five kilometres away. That is measured from a point 2 meters above sea level, which is more or less exactly my height when I stand on the shoreline of southern Gotland and look out over the Baltic. I assume it is impossible to reach the horizon; it is like chasing the end of the rainbow, a physical impossibility. But still, we cannot resist trying to reach that which always escapes us in the same pace as we are approaching it, like the mirage. I observe and paint the birds through my telescope and sometimes I get the feeling of having lessened the distance to the point, the line which we all see but does not actually exist, the horizon. The distance to it may be constant at any given point over the sea, but we can affect the location of that point, we can lower the eyes. The distance to the horizon decreases when one lies down really close to the ground and what seemed remote can suddenly appear very near, like the treasure trove at the end of the rainbow. When I feel in close contact with both myself and the birds I am painting, I sometimes sense a point which, like the horizon, perhaps is an illusion, a point or place where more unites us humans and birds than separates us. That is where I want to be.

This book is based on the catalogue which was produced in connection with an exhibition in Germany at ”Landesmuseum für Natur und Mensch” in Oldenburg summer 2008. The exhibition and catalogue mainly show works from 2002 onwards but are partly retrospective, containing illustrations from my field guides and work from my youth. For this edition I have, however, changed the format somewhat; replaced illustrations, added more comments and given the book another title. Thematically, it has more in common with the book *Birds and Light* which

also functioned as a catalogue for a retrospective exhibit at Prins Eugens Waldemarsudde in Stockholm 2002. I have avoided work which was reproduced in that or previous books except for some illustrations from my field guide *Birds of Europe with North Africa and the Middle East* (1992). It is my hope that the older illustrations, the youthful work and the ornithological studies can bring out the rest of the material in full relief. Most of it centres on birds and their enviroment. The paintings mirrors well in which habitats that I find most of my inspiration: the Sea, Shorelines, Coastal Meadows and Arctic tundras

I would first of all like to thank Peter Reimers who was curator and initiator of the German exhibition and Mamoun Fansa, the director of the museum in Germany, publisher of the original catalogue and author of its foreword. The exhibition titled *Wo Erde und Himmel sich berühren /Where Heaven and Earth Touch* is shown at a further six museums in Denmark, Austria and Germany during autumn 2008 until January 2010. I would also like to thank those who have contributed with texts; Adam Duncan Harris, Kent Ullberg and Fredrik Sjöberg. Christer Jonson, with his rare insight into book typography, has helped me with the design. Bill Ingemarsson and Marie Svärd-Husu at Fälth & Hässler in Värnamo have been very helpful and patient. And last but not least, I must thank my family who coach me in various ways and help me come down softly when I am all revved up.

LARS JONSSON
Hamra September 2008

Lars Jonsson: The Beauty of Nature

ADAM DUNCAN HARRIS, PH.D.

Painting and drawing from life is part of my philosophy,
in fact it is my philosophy.

LARS JONSSON

WHEN ASKED about Jonsson's place in American art, Maria Hajic at the Gerald Peters Gallery in Santa Fe, New Mexico, replied that among knowledgeable collectors, he is in the upper echelon of artists working today. She also noted that he is recognized at two prominent American art museums that focus on wildlife, The Leigh Yawkey Woodson Art Museum and the National Museum of Wildlife Art.[1] Knowledge about Jonsson and his work in the United States does not approach what it is in Sweden, but, with each successful year, his reputation as a fine artist grows.[2] The publication of this book will, without doubt, enhance his reputation as new audiences have the opportunity to view his work.

The art of Lars Jonsson is appreciated by a dedicated cadre of collectors, admirers, and museums who are drawn to his work because of the undeniably beautiful nature of his paintings. Beauty as a quality is an aspect long upheld as the pinnacle in art. While today some artists challenge our notions of what beautiful is, others, like Jonsson, embrace the beautiful as a guiding principal. But he is not painting beauty for beauty's sake, his canvases are not merely surface-level, conventional depictions of subjects we all might find pretty. There is a distinct difference between pretty and beautiful, for beauty can be found in objects that are decidedly not pretty. To even attempt to capture the beauty of nature, in all of its varied splendor, requires more thought, more time, more energy than most artists are willing to invest, but, to Jonsson, this investment is part and parcel of what it means to be an artist. He also has the talent to realize his vision, as Robert Peck, Curator of Art and Artifacts at The Academy of Natural Sciences of Philadelphia, noted, "Jonsson seems to have an almost instinctive understanding of the anatomy, behavior, and habitat of the birds he depicts. The ease of his style is a natural gift, which makes his paintings appear deceptively effortless. In fact, each composition is supported by decades of meticulous study and a life of immersion in the natural world."[3] Jonsson's work is borne of a deep appreciation, even infatuation, with nature. The combination of the words "beautiful nature" adequately conveys in words what Jonsson achieves on canvas, but only if the complex nature of beauty is understood.

Influences

As a young artist and naturalist, Jonsson was influenced by Gunnar Brusewitz and Harald Wiberg whose drawings and watercolors were widely published at the time in Sweden. Jonsson's international reputation as a bird painter started with his first series of bird guides, published 1976–81, which he wrote and illustrated. Several field guide artists impacted Jonsson's development, notably Roger Tory Peterson, with his work in *Birds of Britain and Europe* published in Sweden in 1957. Later, bird illustrations by Arthur Singer, Don Eckelberry and Robert Gillmor all influenced the Jonsson. He, however, cites Leo-Paul Robert, Louis Agassiz Fuertes and Robert Verity Clem as being among the most important influences he had while working on his field guides. Later in his career, he came to appreciate John James Audubon who has the greatest reputation in America, lauded by art museums and natural history museums, alike, for his monumental, four-volume *Birds of America* portfolio. The rest of these artists are known to varying degrees, but most are familiar to anyone who uses a field guide for identifying birds. What links them is their dedication to the accurate depiction of birdlife. Renderings for field guides are an

18 underappreciated part of the art historical cannon. The ongoing interest in this field, even in the age of photography, is substantial and worthy of further study. Part of the challenge for the artist is to create one drawing that will represent an entire species, narrowing variation down to capture the essence of that animal, which is no easy feat.

Anyone who sees Jonsson's watercolor or oil paintings, as opposed to his field guide illustrations, will realize that there is a much more painterly side to his work. This side was influenced by some of the most renowned names in 19ᵗʰ and 20ᵗʰ century art. Jonsson cites Diego Velázquez, Anders Zorn, John Singer Sargent, and Joaquin Sorolla as some of his favorite historic artists. In addition, Jonsson notes influences from the east, including Isaac Levitan, Ilya Repin, and Abram Arkhipov, Russian painters belonging to a group called The Wanderers. In the late 1800s, The Wanderers broke free of a restrictive art establishment to create more personal work. They were social realists, celebrating regular people and folk ways of life. They were also experimenting with light, color, and composition in a manner that paralleled the French Impressionists. Jonsson, in particular, likes their compositions and handling of light and drama. It is no surprise that he is drawn to this group of artists who were taking a close look at the world around them and conveying their impressions of it in a personal manner. Among animal artists, Jonsson has a whole other set of influences, but the Swede Bruno Liljefors is his biggest hero. Liljefors, too, spent much time out in nature, observing its changes and recording his impressions. Jonsson noted that it is complicated to be a Swede, standing on the shoulders of this major predecessor. While it is difficult to get around that shared heritage, with shared landscapes and subjects always at hand, Jonsson has been able to differentiate himself to create his own, individual body of work.

In terms of contemporary artists, Jonsson appreciates the work of Andrew Goldsworthy. Goldsworthy's compositions in nature, whether they are an arrangement of similarly shaped rocks or a pattern of leaves that shows the variegated colors of nature, highlight something about the natural world that the ordinary person might not notice; they enhance the beauty of nature by making it more apparent. Though Jonsson's work is much different than Goldsworthy's, the connection between them is quite clear. Jonsson's drive to honestly present his own vision and experience of nature can serve a similar purpose as Goldsworthy's; it can help people see the beauty and diversity of the world in a new light.

Art and Illustration

Art and illustration are sometimes posed as opposites, especially by artists and art historians, but Jonsson navigates this perceived divide with great ease. His initial artistic success came from his field guide illustrations. For him, creating those pieces was akin to attending art school. Jonsson was not admitted into the prestigious Royal Academy of Art, so had to learn on his own. Classically, an art academy education provided a strict regimen of classes, beginning with drawing from plasters. After a year of honing that skill, students began drawing the living figure before advancing to painting on canvas. Jonsson received a similarly rigorous initiation into art by working on various avian field guides. Field guide illustrations must be incredibly precise and require detailed, careful study in order to faithfully reproduce the dominant characteristics of each sometimes very similar bird. For Jonsson, creating these illustrations made him do the difficult work that has served as the foundation for many a successful artist.

When asked, "Where is the artist in illustration?" Jonsson responded, "Even in illustrating field guides, where you are limited in what you can do, any image still has the mark of the artist who created it." A Jonsson goldfinch is different from a Fuertes goldfinch to anyone familiar with each artist's work. Trying to achieve something new in the field, Jonsson attempted to invigorate his birds, to add small details that would make them come alive, but this was difficult given the strict field guide format. In a guide, people look for a readily identifiable type, generic enough to help them identify an individual of a given species. They are not looking for an artist's interpretation of the bird, the emotional characteristic of art is sublimated. Jonsson noted that Japanese ink drawings are similar to field guide illustration. "There are strict rules and you have to learn your trade very well. Very small, refined differences made things move forward. The Japanese culture being very strict, regular people were not allowed to express much personality in their daily lives. Small differences in your work as opposed to that of you master could be very effective. The same is true in illustration."

The challenge of creating something new in illustration clearly engages Jonsson, but the challenge of creating something new without the field guide strictures has taken him to another level.

Observation, Emotion, Art, Connection

Jonsson ponders why people are still fascinated by Audubon. He said, "There is something about his total passion and life story, a drive that you can read out of the paintings or prints today. After all, it is communication – you communicating with someone else – the presence of the artist addressing something to you as a viewer." This basic, communicative aspect of art is at the core of Jonsson's philosophy. At some point, it does not matter whether the artist is accurately communicating the plumage of a bird in a field guide or is sharing a deeper emotion on canvas. They are parts of greater whole. However, that is not to say that Jonsson treats painting and illustration in the same way. The question of how to move away from the purely representational in wildlife art intrigues him. The goal for him is not merely to create an appealing work of art, but to visually understand what he is looking at and be able to communicate that understanding to viewers, and that, as was mentioned above, approaches the beautiful.

Jonsson's art is based on careful study of nature as well as constant practice, in the form of field sketching. When asked about the role his sketches play, he responded, "The work found in the sketch books is extremely central for me. That work is the basis of my personal philosophy of art. The way the hand-eye-brain connection works is crucial for a visual artist. It is my belief that a wildlife artist has to draw from life. Drawing from life is practice, just like a violin player has to practice. Drawing is about developing the sensitivity of the eye and developing the ability to record and capture distinct moments.

Basically, all traditional training stresses drawing from life. Life-drawing is not only about learning anatomy, but is also about honing your own skills, to be more perceptive, to be more sensitive."

Mastering the ability to capture a moment convincingly on paper or canvas is central to the creation of a great work of art. Many have the ability to copy a photograph, but few take the time to go beyond that rote activity to be truly creative; it is difficult and it takes a lot of practice. The knowledge that comes from constant practice finds fruition in the finished canvas. Being able to sketch confidently allows the artist the freedom to create and not to simply copy; that ability distinguishes the artist from the copyist. Jonsson said, "It is easy to have good photos and to want to paint something that looks nice, but that usually makes for uninteresting results." He continued, "Art should open up your eyes, be a tool to understand the world around you." The great artist can paint a picture of something the viewer may have seen many times before, but elicit a fresh response or a new emotion simply in the way he or she composed their painting.

Jonsson called his creations on paper or canvas "emotional journeys into representation." Each day, particularly in nature, the journey differs. The more time he spends in careful observation, trying to dissolve nature into different elements - light, shadow, atmosphere – the greater the personal involvement and the more he feels he understands. He said of observing nature, "Today there might be more humidity, or the deer are traveling down the mountains, or the wind is blowing in a different direction. It is so crucial to use your eyes to observe and understand." When he gets completely involved, he will sit for hours, trying to decipher the patterns and rhythms of nature happening all around him. For Jonsson, this activity of paying close attention to nature is a fundamental element of his art. He said that connection with nature is "something primitive and elemental, and it brings pleasure." That pleasure, that deep level of involvement, comes out in his paintings - a communication, a connection, from artist to viewer. With that deep level of understanding and interaction with nature, true art can emerge.

Jonsson also appreciates the challenge of sketching new subjects, or of sketching the same subjects on a new day. "I have said several times that I paint what I see, not what I know, and the act of drawing and painting ad hoc creates new perspectives, while painting what you know is repetitive, and that is why I love to draw in the field." That interaction between artist and nature creates an intensity that sparks the imagination. Jonsson calls the heightened level of attention, excitement, adrenaline, and alertness that coincides with a wildlife sighting "the vibrating now," which also describes the energy directed by the observer at the observed. Jonsson said of watching animals, "Experiencing wildlife is very much about the moment, *the vibrating now*, when a bird or other animal appears in front of you, turns its head, feeds, stalks, or kills. It is about the moment. Capturing that moment is not only about making things look right, it is about creating that feeling of presence. Commercial illustration visualizes someone else's story, it puts things together so that you can see it and understand it rather than feeling it. Art is about emotions, to create a space where viewers are brought in contact with their own emotions."

Jonsson relates to Einstein's conceptualization of the spiritual aspects of cosmic creation, which says, in a nutshell, that the whole universe, whoever created it, is in and of itself an engaging thing to contemplate. Jonsson said, "It's a wonderful experience to try to understand it, to observe it, to think about it." He tries to take his talent as an observer, as a painter, and see how much he can do with it, how much about life he can express and understand in a rendering of a single bird. This becomes a very personal exercise. "For me," Jonsson added, "the act of painting in the field or in front of a live animal is about dismantling my personal shield, to be in direct contact with my inner being, to make a footprint of my personal emotions in the moment of observation. The emotions do not have to be on a grand scale; they may be very small moments of enlightenment, or joy, but all represent something true and that is transferred to the canvas."

The ability to honestly capture an emotion such as joy or enlightenment on canvas in a meaningful way is extremely difficult. One of Jonsson's watercolors of shorebirds can communicate something about nature to a whole range of people, many of whom may have never seen that type of shorebird, or any shorebird at all. The point is that his renderings do more than record a particular bird on a particular day, they are more than snapshots of a scene. Jonsson's paintings communicate something much greater about nature and our place within it. Jonsson's paintings take a scene and present it to us in a way that opens our eyes to a new appreciation for the natural beauty that surrounds us.

ADAM DUNCAN HARRIS has been the Curator of Art at the National Museum of Wildlife Art in Jackson Hole, Wyoming since 2000. He recceived a Bachelor´s degree from Brown University before continuing on to the University of Wyoming for a Master´s degree in American Studies. He finished his academic studies at the University of Minnesota, where he recieved a Ph.D in Art History, focusing in American Art and Film.

1. The Leigh Yawkey Woodson Art Museum is located in Wausau, Wisconsin, and the National Museum of Wildlife Art, where the author is Curator of Art, is located in Jackson, Wyoming, U.S.A.
2. Interview with Maria Hajic, February 10, 2008.
3. Email correspondence with Robert Peck, February 25, 2008.

About Lars Jonsson

KENT ULLBERG, NA

I N THIS book we can read about Lars Jonsson in essays by a distinguished scholar from an Art museum and a cultural critic and from two different national perspectives.

I would like to talk about Lars from the point of view of a fellow artist.

We know Lars is one of the most treasured artists in Sweden. I grew up and studied in Sweden, but I have lived and worked in many parts of the world, including seven years in Africa and the last thirty years in the USA. So in addition to my pride in Lars as a Swede, I'd like to address his international reputation. Stated quite simply and up front, amongst us artists working in the wildlife genre, Lars is recognized as the foremost bird painter. His influence has been tremendous for many years now and artists crop up all over attempting the "Lars Jonsson look". Yes, that has become an expression amongst wildlife artists.

I first became aware of Lars' work as a staff member of the National Museum of Natural History in Stockholm, when Lars had his first one-man show there at the age of 15. It caused a sensation among the museum's professionals. Artists and scientists alike were in total disbelief that work of such beauty, maturity and accuracy could have been created by a 15 year old. However, Lars has never fitted any conventional molds: when at seven years old his proud parents submitted his work to a children's art-competition, the were accused of fraud. The judges didn't believe it to be the work of a child.

Then, as we fast forward to Lars still in his twenties, having published five bird books in 7 languages with the most beautiful illustrations ever seen, you realize again Lars doesn't quite fit the molds.

The foremost recognition in the field of avian art, "The Master Wildlife Artist Award" is given by an American institution, the Leigh Yawkey Woodson Art Museum in Wisconsin.

By definition a Master is normally an older mature artist, and the award has been given to some of the greatest names. In 1988 Lars was only thirty-six, the youngest ever to be so honoured. At that time the recipients were proposed and voted upon by all the previous masters. It's significant when one realizes the prestige of the artists involved. Roger Tory Peterson, Sir Peter Scott, Don Eckelberry, Robert Bateman, a. o., expressed in personal conversation that there was no question about Lars's candidacy.

The most unusual aspect about Lars, however, is his work, his approach to his subject matter in the field. I have had the privilege of accompanying him on field trips, watching him paint birds in many different biotopes, from the shores of the Gulf Coast to the Rocky Mountains. It is a singularly amazing and moving experience. Lars has the most sensitive eye I've ever seen.

Because of the often "en passant" experiences we have with our subjects, the field work of most wildlife artists, myself included, consists of photography and sometimes sketches and notes, desperately trying to record as much information as possible. Finished work like painting and sculptures is normally done in the studio. Lars however paints beautiful and sensitive watercolors of birds in the field. It appears as if he has one eye in the telescope and one on the watercolor pad while the paint flows like magic; but of course Lars has the most incredible knowledge of his subject matter, both scientific and aesthetic, gained from what would normally be several lifetimes spent in the field.

Interestingly, the very root-word for "art" in our Germanic languages is: knowledge, ability. In fact, one of Sweden's most famous and beloved painters

Anders Zorn (1860–1920), loved to quote a saying in German: "Kunst kommt aus können". Ernest Hemingway often expressed to write "truly" you have to know your subject matter intimately. This is still the most powerful advise for artists in any media, and one which I have tried to live by. However, in his field paintings, Lars goes beyond even this idea.

Years ago he said something that shook me up, and which I still find very profound: "To see truly in the field, you must totally trust your eyes and forget: what you know" I understand this as seeing innocently, as for the first time, no editing or "fixing stuff" based on prior knowledge. This is coming from a man who probably knows more about avian subjects than anybody alive.

I believe this striving to see "truly" and honestly, every time, is what gives Lars' paintings their power. His work transcends subject matter into the universal and sublime. His audience feels his absolute honesty, in fact he is the most honest artist I know.

A native of Sweden, KENT ULLBERG, born in 1945, is recognized as one of the world's foremost wildlife sculptors. He studied at the Swedish Konstfack School of Art in Stockholm, and at museums in Germany, France and the Netherlands. He lived in Botswana, Africa for seven years and served there for the last four years as curator at the Botswana National Museum. Since 1974 he lives in Texas and Colorado, USA. He is best known for his monumental sculptures and has exhibited worldwide. His work is represented in major public collections.

On the Subject of Beauty

FREDRIK SJÖBERG

*Does there not exist a high ridge where
the mountainside of scientific knowledge joins
the opposite slope of artistic imagination?*
VLADIMIR NABOKOV

MY INTENTION is not to tell you about all the tree stumps and chairs I have sat on. It would surely be an unbearable story. Only about two of them, no more; one tree stump and one chair, with half a lifetime in between. Only then can we approach the riddle of Lars Jonsson's unique position on the stage of contemporary art. Truly, a mystery. Or not? We shall see.

The tree stump stands in my childhood or, to put it more precisely, in a sparse pine forest on the shore of the Baltic Sea, a cycling distance from the small town, on the outskirts of which I grew up. I had been a bird-watcher for a few days. I had been collecting beetles, butterflies and other insects for years; I had busied myself with them, and, at one time, botany had taken up the whole of my summer holidays. But for some reason I had decided to turn to birds. Possibly, because I wanted company – I can't quite remember. Perhaps it was simply because I had just been present-ed with my first field guide. I was by now also old enough to be allowed to borrow the pair of Beck Kassel German binoculars from my father. It was a beautiful day in April, I was on my own. I sat there as quiet as a mouse. Waiting.

Of course, I already knew something about the bird fauna of the region. As long as I could remember there had been a red-painted bird table in front of our kitch-en window; the common tits I recognized, just like the fieldfare and the tree creeper, the green woodpeckers, the nuthatches, the bullfinches. Perhaps even some others as well. However, they had not been anything more than extras in a much larger performance, a con-tinuing spectacle in which squirrels, deer and the occasional fox played the major parts. I had never devoted myself to more detailed studies. Only watch-ing, never seeing. Yet now, the time had come, and in the trees around me a scattered and mixed flock of small birds was romping around. I learned the call of the crested tit that day and saw more goldcrests than I was able to count. But it was something else which led me to experience that certain euphoria which one feels when, for the first time, you really make contact with a bird.

Banal, of course, and difficult to explain. Almost private. A coal tit. My first. It came very close and was so feverishly busy looking for edible insects among the pine needles, that I had all the time in the world to study it with my binoculars. How strange. The bird was as small as a blue tit, but its plumage reminded me more of a great tit, even though the colour was not right. I leafed through my bird book, starting at the back, and found a convincing answer. A coal tit. Without any doubt. The feeling was so sensational that even now, almost forty years later, I am unable to see a coal tit in a forest without feeling some of that first wild joy of discovery.

As I said, we have to take a detour to understand Lars Jonsson. The artist and the phenomenon.

The chair was on a stage. In the audience there was an expectant muttering. I was nervous. It was in September 2006 during the bookfair in Göteborg. I had just published my book "The Art of Escape" on the watercolour artist Gunnar Mauritz Widforss (1879–1934), who had fallen into oblivion, and my publisher had arranged a large seminar. We were sup-posed to be talking about art. And since the poor people who arrange seminars for overcrowded book-fairs sleep badly at night - because they worry about the sense of drama and possibly, a bored audience resulting from the lack of the same - they had placed a second chair on the stage. On this chair they had installed a most lively artist; it was Lars Vilks, the *enfant terrible* of the Swedish art scene, a man who is as notorious as Lars Jonsson is famous. His aesthetics, more than most, pay tribute to the role of the artist as a troublemaker and commentator of society, preferred mode the one of the rabulist. His colossal sculpture is legendary: made from driftwood, it can be seen in a nature reserve on the 'Kulla berg' in Skåne, Southern Sweden. Just as legendary as his clever move to prevent the authorities from taking down this illegal pile of planks by selling it to Joseph Beuys (1921-1986). We won't go into it in more detail. Actually, I only have a somewhat vague memory of this performance in Göteborg. To be honest, I was at the end of my tether with nervousness. However, I still remember a couple of things, for example that the background behind our chairs consisted of a huge screen where two images, two book jackets, were shown throughout our conversation. The one, from my book, reproduced a very beautiful and very carefully composed watercolour, painted in the 1920s by Gunnar Widforss, showing the Half Dome mountain in the Yosemite Valley, California. Yes, in the end he emigrated across the Atlantic and is being celebrated in the USA to this day, as one of great painters of the American wilderness. Only in his native country has he been forgotten, the poor fellow.

Be that as it may, the second jacket belonged, appropriately, to one of Lars Vilks' books. The title of which – *How to become a contemporary artist within three days* – was all you could see on there, since the jacket consisted of pure typography without any pictures. This was our starting point. I asked: Can we consider one of the pictures behind us as art? Whereupon the friendly Vilks, well versed in art theory and its contexts, started going on about something we had known for some time – that nowadays art can be everything, apart from naturalistic landscape painting. Especially watercolours. These were not pieces of art, but illustrations. I had hardly hoped for a better start. Happily, we started giving as good as we were getting, and I think, as time went by, the audience also had some food for thought – not least, because we had complicated the question even further by touching on Ansel Adams (1902– 1984). His well known black and white photos of the same mountain as painted by Widforss, and also taken from the same angle, are unequivocally regarded as great art.

When both were still alive, Widforss was the artist and Adams the illustrator. Now, it was the other way round. As if the camera requires more skill than the paintbrush. The audience was moving about on their seats. The odd embarrassed laugh. Yes, you must not take it too seriously. Debates on the subject of right and wrong in the world of art often develop into a splitting of hairs. Since I was the outsider in all the important aspects, a fleeting observer on a short visit, the matter did not bother me any further after the seminar had ended and the audience had gone home. I had, by pure chance, discovered Widforss, recognized his talent, his wonderful eye for the nuances of landscapes. That was enough for me. I am not a person who gets worked up when somebody wants to shout loudly and stir up outrage in the name of art, or possibly even put a pillow case over a Parliament building. Each to his own.

Only later, when I became engrossed in the case of Lars Jonsson, did I return to my thoughts on the stage of contemporary art. Which is not particularly large. Let me remind you at this point that Sweden is a small country as far as the number of inhabitants is concerned. Maybe that makes it special. There is not much room in the limelight for many at the same time, either individuals or –isms. Sometimes it is said, and I think there is some truth in it, that the cause for the lack of generosity – bordering on cannibalism - which determines the relationships between the artists, is connected to this sad circumstance. To attain a place in the sun you need to throw somebody else out, or, at least, block their path. The pleasure of opposition, which has determined the artistic life in our country for more than a hundred years, is, above all, a protest, which is directed against other artists and other stylistic ideals than the ones setting the tone at the time. This is regrettable, but also understandable. The fine arts have never enjoyed a well-funded mass audience of the kind experienced by literature and later, music. And for contemporary conceptual art the available share is even smaller. This is why patrons and institutions have always been so important. Competition is murderous.

As early as the 1880s, when the painters trained in Paris returned home, intoxicated by new ideas and theories, their opposition had the character of an internal settling of scores, which was certainly not unjustified. The old-fashioned studio painting with its roots in the overloaded equilibrist studios of the Düsseldorf school of painting, had got stuck within its own formalism and sluggish bureaucracy. The fresh breeze from France had long been craved for, just like some decades later, when, headed by Isaac Grünewald (1889–1946), the first students of Matisse turned up and stole the show from their old opponents. As a result, the national romanticism and symbolism of the turn of the century were banished to the history books. The definitive breakthrough of the modern age happened quite late in Sweden, but, when the modernists finally made it onto the stage in the 1940s, all light fell upon them. As I said, a small country.

Of course, I am simplifying, but you need to understand: We have to find the solution to a riddle. Lars Jonsson. How it is possible that he, this Jonsson – a painter of birds, who counts the Düsseldorf trained Bruno Liljefors (1860–1939) among his influences, who was for decades a favourite among elderly gentlemen – stands up there, in the middle of the stage, untouched and celebrated as one of the truly great artists of our time in this period of thought-provoking video installations and interactive definition of space? A talent, mostly self-taught, who is continuously depicting birds from nature. Can we be more wrong?

Certainly, the path to recognition in the salons was not a simple one. In 1972 Lars Jonsson found himself not being accepted into the Swedish academy of art, something that probably hurt his pride. On the other hand, we need to be grateful that it forced him to find his own way, not least, if we remember what the teaching at the academy was like at the time; perhaps not exactly like an Albanian people's front, but deeply rooted within the political movements and actions of its time. I don't think it is out of place to say that Jonsson would have lost some of his distinctiveness in this environment (he was, after all, only 19 years old) or perhaps something which then developed into his distinctive style. He had a precocious talent as a child, that much is true, but many children have this kind of talent and never manage to refine it.

His field guides became his university. The commission by a large publisher to do no fewer than five bird guides, published between 1976 and 1980, became in many ways his apprenticeship, albeit a difficult one. The one who seeks recognition as an artist should avoid doing field guides; and the one who, on top of this, accepts commissions for illustrations on an almost industrial scale, should be prepared for a career as a painter who commands little respect. In this context I occasionally waste a thought on Gottfrid Kallstenius (1861–1943), one of the painting colleagues of Bruno Liljefors around the turn of the century. One of the best, but he made the mistake (not his only one) of writing a handbook on oil painting, while, at the same time, offering his services as an advisor to the paint manufacturer, Becker. It did not take long for the foundations of his later fame to be laid, with phrases like "too interested in technical details". That he was one of the best landscape painters has been forgotten. A shortsighted pedant, almost a scientist. As we all know, something that does not go well with the myth of the romantic artist.

Here, at exactly this point, we will start our journey towards a possible solution to our riddle. Not with the artist, but with the scientist Lars Jonsson. The man who sits with his binoculars and his easel on the shore and says; "I paint what I see, not what I know". I will come back to this statement. Above all, it interests me, because it is probably not the whole truth, possibly, only a partial truth.

However, Jonsson is not a scientist in the formal sense – he is self-taught – but his knowledge of ornithology commands great respect in the circles of strict empiricists and professional experts. His intensive work on his field guides – some of them were later revised and summarized in the volume *The Birds of Europe with North Africa and the Middle East* (1992) which was translated into eleven languages – led to a familiarity with the innumerable nuances according to which species can be distinguished. With this, he became part of the long and glorious tradition of illustrators of the natural sciences, amongst whom we find names like the Americans John James Audubon (1785–1851) and Louis Agassiz Fuertes (1874–1927), the German Joseph Wolf (1820–1899) and the Finnish brothers Magnus (1805–1868) and Wilhelm von Wright (1810–1887), to name but a few. Lars Jonsson was meant to bring this genre back to life by his persistent illustrations from nature using spectives, and also by using at times an impressionistic trademark paired with a distinct individualization of his motifs. Yet at this point of his career he is closely tied to a discipline, which is intimately connected with biological science. As we will see, he developed from there, but, like all basic training, the years of apprenticeship have left their indelible marks.

This is a strong point; but from the perspective of art sociology, from which I consider Lars Jonsson's work out of pure pleasure, it might as well have been a millstone round his neck. Still, I am fairly sure that the scientific aspect is more of an explanation for his success as an artist on the stage. To further illustrate my point, I suggest a short detour into literature, accompanied by an Englishman and a Russian.

Almost fifty years have gone by since the British physicist and novelist C.P. Snow (1905–1980) wrote his famous essay *The two cultures* – a text which was not originally intended to be an essay, but a lecture, held on May 7th 1959 in Cambridge. The lecture on the two cultures immediately became a universal term, which also developed a life of its own removed from its original context. Snow's essay was initially a pamphlet on educational policies which dealt with academics, especially in England, not talking to each other. Instead, they pull faces at each other across the gulf, which separates the natural sciences from the humanities. Especially this last group – Snow calls them *the literary intellectuals* – has, in his eyes, not the slightest interest in understanding what natural scientists deal with. This, in turn, damages the prosperity of the country as far as the competition with the USA and the Soviet Union is concerned. Wafflers! That is what he calls his adversaries. Snow touched on a sore point. At the time of flowering capitalism, when the physicists were beginning to change the world, it was indeed worrying that great groups within the intelligentsia had only a vague idea of what was happening, and probably had no appreciation for the methods of natural sciences. The natural scientists themselves were no model pupils either, and times have changed since then. Today, the role of physics is less noticeable within the structure of society, and, during the last fifty years quantum physics, at least, has been reconciled with philosophy. Thus the gulf is no longer as deep, not even in England. But this term lives on – The two cultures – and today is a distressingly current one within the relationship between the humanities and the scientific discipline that is trying to change the world – I mean biology. I do not necessarily mean the knowledge of birds, but more molecular genetics and other biological arts of engineering. The problem is evident, everybody knows about it, and many hope for a dialogue between the worlds of research and cultural life. The theatre of science and similar projects are becoming more and more prevalent, even if these attempts seem artificial, as is often the case with publicly prescribed art. Still, they are an expression of a wide-reaching effort for a better appreciation. Scientists and artists show certain similarities where creativity is concerned, and, when they meet in the same person something strange will happen, something that no project sponsorship can manage. If we look at it from this angle, Lars Jonsson is a living answer to the rhetorical question that the author Vladimir Nabokov (1899–1977) – himself an outstanding entomologist in addition to his controversial literary work – formulated in the New York Book Review. It is "Does there not exist a high ridge where the mountainside of scientific knowledge joins the opposite slope of artistic imagination?"

We could easily continue our optimistic analysis and classify Lars Jonsson according to a different, more current context. Namely, as a member of the group of contemporary artists who consider it their task to design the ecological crisis, the threat to nature and finally the survival of humankind. Yet we can do without that. He is part of this group, but only indirectly. By painting wild birds within an apparently virginal environment instead of reveling in oil spills and other effective blackness, he makes a contribution to laying the groundwork – the sense of, and the love for, nature. On these foundations one can build an enduring contribution to questions of ecology. That is not his intention, but only a side effect of the drama he presents us with. We will come back to this. However, since we have to cross the minefield first, the minefield of what beauty is, we shall have to wait a little longer.

First, a reflection on birds as a legitimate motif. The expression may seem strange, but at all times artists had to fight against, or adapt to, unspoken standards that determined which motif was acceptable. For a long time the church practically had a monopoly in the field of fine arts, but since the renaissance freedom has been progressing, slowly but surely. Profane landscapes and people, alternately.

In the same way, the horizon of animal painting has expanded. Let us linger for a moment on people – not chiefly on the legions of ample, naked women from the sleeping Venus to the glossy porn of our time, who, for reasons easily understood, became a popular motif - but on children. It is a somewhat complicated story which centers around the topic of intolerance, dependent on the gender.

Someone who is interested in the pecking order on the art stage can usefully study the envious reactions which inhibited the female Swedish artists of the past century. To analyse this in detail, would take us far away from our subject. Therefore I would like to restrict myself to the choice of motif, which varied widely, of course, but is still typical if we remind ourselves that Sigrid Hjerten (1855–1948), Mollie Faustman (1883–1966), Vera Nilsson (1888–1979) and many others, painted their own or other people's children, which set them apart from their male colleagues and which did not really count as art. Many years later a few of them, too few of them, gained some measure of recognition which they would have deserved much earlier – partly because times were changing for the better, partly because children had become a legitimate motif. It was much more than just the choice of motif which kept these women insignificant, but we must not underestimate its importance. Also, it is definitely part of our story, because a similar phenomenon happened to Lars Jonson at the beginning of his career. He only painted birds. That did not really count. I may be wrong, as always, but even as far as this is concerned, I seem to detect a changing attitude. Perhaps it is more about Jonsson's increasingly more explicit descriptions of the actual meetings with birds as individuals, than about a change in prevalent taste. That is not so crucial. An indisputable fact is, and remains, that his painting developed from the summarizing descriptions of species into something like portrait painting. This characteristic feature had been there from the start and was perhaps his most important contribution to the revival of the genre. But he has accelerated this individualization to such an extent that at times the observer stands there as if in front of a mirror.

Mind you, I am not talking about anthropomorphisms. It is not that Lars Jonsson attributes human sensations to the birds in his paintings, but, he makes identification possible at any time - identification of a kind which does not demand a greater ornithological knowledge of the observer than he could achieve by looking at a bird table or by going on a walk along a beach. Then suddenly, he is a painter rather than a painter of birds. What is his secret?

At this point it might be advisable to pay another brief visit to the science of biology. During the last four decades that have gone by since Lars Jonsson first appeared in public with his paintings, a lot of changes have taken place. The greatest breakthrough by far has been in evolutionary biology and is known under the term *synthetic theory of evolution*, more commonly known as neo-darwinism, developed by, amongst others, the German-American biologist Ernst Mayr (1905–2005). By connecting Darwin's theory of evolution with modern genetics, he and other scientists reached the groundbreaking conclusion that evolution is effective by natural selection on an individual level, and not, as formerly believed, on the level of the species. This already happened in the 1940s but, outside of universities, the theory did not create any noteworthy impact until the English writer Richard Dawkins popularized synthesis and its consequences in his 1976 bestseller *The Selfish Gene*.

Today this way of thinking permeates all branches of biology. Yes, not only those; the idea has penetrated human consciousness in such a way that its core influences our whole view of nature. It is not the species which competes for space and occasions to procreate, but individuals outside the species. A shift in paradigms in the wider sense of the word – which has certainly introduced something radically new, as far as observing individual birds is concerned. The coal tit, when busy looking for food, is part of a complex ecological network, a greater context. Yet, in the first place, it is not a mechanical representative of the species coal tit, but an individual with its own agenda. It is possible that Lars Jonsson would have developed his art in the direction of portrait painting even without these ideas, but I believe that they are of great significance to me and to other observers fascinated by the twinkle in his models' eyes.

In the same breath it must be pointed out, that the examination of the individual within the context of neo-darwinism is only a flicker on the surface of an ancient relationship between humankind and animal, in everyday life just as in art.

The British writer and art critic John Berger is looking at this relationship in more detail in his collection of essays *Ways of Seeing* (1980) and convincingly submits the theory that animals, even before the time of cave paintings, had their place within the imagination of people. Above all, as harbingers and prophesies, less as venison worthy of hunting. Today, according to Berger, in the lavish *Walt Disney World* of our modern society, there is no source more important to the imagery than animals. They are omnipresent. Identification happens almost automatically. If Lars Jonsson had been driven from early childhood by the tremendous desire to study and paint mushrooms and toadstools instead of birds, he would never have come near the stage – no matter how skilled he would have proven himself in illustrating everything from the *Russula integra* to the *Cortinarius collinitus*. Perhaps he could have passed as an artist in the most precious sense of the word – if he had concentrated on eating certain mushrooms (of the hallucinogenic kind) and had then banned his inner visions on big, colourful easels in some deserted factory building – but not as an illustrator of field guides. I am sure about that. It is to do with the fact that the identification between observer and motif is more difficult, even impossible, and that mushrooms are generally completely still. Thus, they lack the ability to flee. This is, as we shall see, of central significance for Lars Jonsson's artistic work.

The painting of cows, once popular all over the world, takes up an interesting intermediate stage in this. There is, or was, a whole group of really good painters, who I would like to study in a lot more detail, time allowing. Strictly specialised painters of cows like Paul Potter (1625–1654) and others, as well as painters of horses and dogs, like George Stubbs (1724–1806) and Johan von Holst (1841–1917), can tell us something about the strange, endless game between humans and animals. The viewpoint can be that of a farmer or of the comrade or, as it happened later with Bruno Liljefors, the viewpoint of a hunter. In Lars Jonsson's case it was initially that of an observer of birds; later, the relationship became more complicated and the picture not quite so simple anymore. Like a mirror. Anyway, we can say that animals in art can achieve a significance which does not come second to human motifs.

Suddenly, the thought pops into my head that we should, at this point, dare follow a side track for a little while, and observe a strange creature which has recently appeared on the Swedish art stage – the roundabout dog.

It all started when the sculptress Stina Opitz received the commission to beautify a roundabout in the Swedish town of Linköping. The sculpture, or rather the installation, titled *Circulation II,* consisted of a gigantic, slanting concrete tire with the same diameter as the roundabout, as well as of a dog, 70 centimetres high, made of white lightweight concrete. It was presented to the public in the spring of 2006. Up to then, the whole thing had been considered an unspectacular event in Swedish cultural life. Normal public art. Regrettably, someone – we do not know who – had the cheek to knock off the concrete dog's head and dispose of it on another roundabout in Mjölby. Now, something interesting happened. Some youths fabricated a new dog out of wood, which they, according to the legend, installed on the roundabout as a protest against vandalism. Because this action resulted in various articles in the local press, creativity was stimulated, and it did not take long until imaginatively made dogs appeared on roundabouts all over Östergötland. The roundabout dog of Östergötland was born, or, as they call it in the international arena, *The Ostrogothian Roundabout Dog.* An artistic success. A much loved and hated pet, distantly related to the shaggy goat Robert Rauschenberg stuck into a car tire at the beginning of the Sixties, and which has since become one of the greatest attractions in the Moderna Museet in Stockholm. As I said, animals have something that it is difficult to resist. Consequently, the making of roundabout dogs quickly became a popular movement. They turned up all over Sweden in their hundreds; they appeared overnight, more or less skilfully made, in all materials and sizes. Soon there were reports that roundabout dogs had been sighted outside of Sweden. No end of this epidemic is in sight, although we have to point out that this, the funniest of all kennels, suffered a setback in the summer of 2007 when Lars Vilks seized the idea. He caused a commotion by presenting a roundabout dog depicting the prophet

Mohammad. At once riots broke out in Pakistan, and Vilks suddenly became world-famous. He gave long interviews on CNN and even managed to persuade the terrorist organization Al Qaida to offer a reward for his head. Some may call this media spectacle art, as if the whole thing was a gigantic installation. Another description for it is nonsense.

Well, I would not have mentioned all this if I had not thought it belonged here.

It does. At least my feeling tells me, that a large section of the European art crowd is fed up with the habitual breaking of taboos and programmatic provocations by contemporary artists. They have to look feverishly for new lines to cross, move further and further to gain the desired effect. Maybe the rioting against everything that can be called holy has not reached the end of the flagpole yet, but, like all revolutions, it shows the tendency to get stuck in dogmatism and empty rhetoric whereupon the whole thing starts afresh: the search for something new.

Lars Jonsson's painting is not a magic formula or even a satisfactory answer to the question where we can find something new. Nevertheless I am convinced that the increasing desire of the art lovers not to be provoked, which we can observe today, gets us closer to the question how it is possible that a painter like him managed not only to conquer the audience, but also to enjoy the doubtful respect normally given to a very different kind of artist in these insecure times. At any rate, his success was almost sensational when Jonsson filled one of our great national art museums (Prince Eugen's Waldemarsudde in Stockholm) with his pictures in the autumn of 2002. The numbers of visitors to the exhibition could hardly have been achieved by any other living artist with his/her roots in the classical tradition of painting.

This can partly be explained by the fact that Lars Jonsson is international in his art, which is very important in a globalised world like ours. The same birds here and there, the same reflections. This does not make him dependent on the, partly national, sounding board which normally limits typical landscape painting. After all, we are all moulded by the landscape we grow up in. Plus, it is hardly a concern of contemporary art to give shape to these fairly romantic memories. It deals with more difficult matters.

Therefore we want to consider what Lars Jonsson

himself says. What does he actually do? "I paint what I see, not what I know." A fundamental programmatic explanation, given some time in the middle of the Nineties, perhaps half as a protest against post modernism, which was slowly getting blue in the face due to lack of oxygen. He has always been generous with explanations, spoken and written, relating to his art. We can say what we like, but he is not a mystic, and therefore his dependency on the direct visual impressions through his face-to-face contact with nature is crystal clear. Larger motifs in oil receive their finishing touches in his studio, but their creation always goes back to sketches captured from nature – pictures of a moment. The subtle iridescence of light and colour, quite fleeting. Hence it is true that Lars Jonsson paints what he sees, but as a programmatic explanation this can cause the wrong impression, and even lets us think of the justified criticism directed against the photographs of Ansel Adams – the creation of art out of something seen in the viewfinder.

Without doubt, Lars Jonsson has seen a lot, a lot more of everything called bird than all the others in the audience. Most of us will discover the one or other reference to encounters of our own in the countryside, and remember a spark of that magic which flourishes in the undergrowth of our childhood. Yet, what does that signify? That we are a secret brotherhood, able to name coal tits even before reaching puberty? Hardly. That is not the point. Such memories have a power of their own, we cannot deny it, and it is good to channel them; but it does not explain the phenomenon. The man on the stage who, even though he only paints birds, manages to pull in the crowds whose knowledge of dunlins, pintails, and lesser black-backed gulls is meagre. It is something different. Something, which Lars Jonsson knows.

First, the fleetingness. A wistful perception, so easy to feel, yet so difficult to see. Lars Jonsson knows a lot about it, and describes it time and again, year by year. Not only because of the simple fact that birds by nature tend to flee, but also by the careful choice of motifs. He does not follow the direct route. On the contrary, most of his pictures are characterized by their almost physical calm. Waiting and calmness. His craft, his technical perfection he might have learned from Bruno Liljefors, but his style, his stroke, are worlds apart from the drama of times gone by.

Times which were often dictated by the influence of a coarse social Darwinism, which turned the fight for survival into the key phrase of identification. Waiting and calmness and watchfulness. Which we recognize, and we know that, but at the same time we feel instinctively that the spell can be broken at any moment. The drama is always there, the fight in our lives and the lives of the birds, but Lars Jonsson has decided to describe the moments preceding it. The fleeting, and thereby exceptional, moment of calmness. Of all of Lars Jonsson's books I am particularly fond of the first two parts of the so-called Gotland-trilogy *Ön/ The island* (1983) and *En dag i maj/One day in May* (1990). In these he consistently tells the same story in an additional, almost epic perspective, as he does in the majority of his individual paintings. The story of what will soon be over and gone. A sandbank appearing for an instant, created by a winter storm, on which the birds come and go, before it once again disappears into the sea. Or, a hectic and seething day in May, when nature on Gotland is as beautiful as never before. An island. A day. Happiness, we could call it. That is the one point.

All of which takes us to the second point, which is so trivial that I resisted saying something about it until now. Yet, it might be the most important one. It is not just about the birds, but about something different. We could call it loneliness. Not the usual loneliness, which we can find in almost all types of art, and which mirrors the basically tragic project that mine, the observer's, life, is but short. No, not this one. No world-weariness. And, of course, I would be an idiot to deny that this is personal. I do not claim that I know the absolute truth as far as these matters are concerned, but I have the certain feeling that Lars Jonsson can reach us in happy moments, without any intermediaries, by creating the loneliness in such a way that it makes us return from it in better shape than before. A step to one side in our hectic times. A breather. Yes, beauty.

I imagine that Lars Jonsson's bird portraits and impressions of Gotland and anywhere else are always a private matter. The value increases, the fewer observers there are. It is best to encounter these paintings by yourself. Which does not turn them into something new and revolutionary, but into something astonishingly unusual on the art stage of our

time – which rests mainly on the fact that the observer is seen by all the other observers and is appreciated due to his good taste. In the end, we put ourselves up on our walls, especially those of us, who call themselves intellectuals and suffer under the heavy yoke of being overambitious, or just worry about doing the wrong thing, to be sidelined. Even Lars Jonsson can be used in contexts like these, as an ornament, a trophy, where the spotlight is on the signature to allay the suspicion the painting could be from one of his imitators. Though I am still of the opinion that the majority of his admirers are seeking something other than vain confirmation. Something a lot more difficult and, at the same time, ridiculously simple. Let us talk about beauty for a moment. International art deals with difficult subjects. Provocative, political pictures of battles and installations in the shadow of *Guernica* alternate with heart wrenching descriptions of more personal battlefields within the geography of body and soul, for which pioneers like Frida Kahlo (1907–1954) paved the way. Difficult subjects, deeply personal, sometimes even dangerous for someone who provokes the wrong Taliban. But difficult as these motifs or topics may be for the individual artist, at least he or she does not need to cope with administrators of personal tastes, who are guarding the stage – due to the formerly arduous aesthetics having become the academically valid ones of today. Today, maltreatments and dystopian visions, ironies, cynicism and political manifestos are the forceful choices within the arts, just as it was previously the national romantic style of the turn of the last century, or shallow historical painting, which was swept away by its opponents when its time came.

As I said, Sweden is a small country and therefore possibly special. After the old attitude towards beauty in the fine arts was written off as out of touch with the times, we had a proper clearout. With all its advantages and drawbacks. It was certainly an advantage that freedom from impeding norms and the necessity for technical skills – which required talent as well as time-consuming finishing – meant that everybody with a little imagination could become an artist, even if not necessarily within three days. But believe me, the drawbacks were predominant. However, since I read not only Lars Vilks, but also August Strindberg (1849–1912), who as early as 1877 wrote the stimulating book *Instructions on how to become an art connoisseur in 60 minutes*, I will refrain from further views on what was lost when contemporary art distanced itself from the fundamental values of beauty, which had been preserved by poets, musicians, architects and others of the same period in the name of syntax, scales and classical proportions.

I would just like to state that a painter, who claims to create something beautiful with his paintbrush – as if that was enough – will do well to follow his own path and to bring along a certain amount of courage. For the simple reason, that it is more difficult today than it has been for a long time, to represent beauty - trivial or not. In this field Lars Jonsson is a pioneer. Perhaps that is how he made it onto the stage, I thought. I looked out of the window. A Great Black-backed Gull high above the lake; the wind is getting up.

FREDRIK SJÖBERG, born 1958 in Västervik, Sweden lives today on Runmarö, an island in the archipelago of Stockholm. Sjöberg is a writer, translator and biologist. He works as a journalist and critic for the Swedish newspaper Svenska Dagbladet. Sjöberg published several books, mainly focusing on scientific issues, lately »Flugfällan« (2004) und »Flyktkonsten« (2006), two essays between literature and prose.

I began drawing birds around the age of four. Birds must have captivated me to the extent that I have been searching for birds in all kinds of perspectives ever since. A neighbour's daughter, who often babysat my brother and me, was genuinely interested in birds, so perhaps it was her who placed a seed. On a sheet from 1957 that my mother saved and on which I drew birds on one side, the main figure is a large, distinct bird which makes me think it was a House Sparrow. On the other side I have also drawn people, with heads more like birds, faces in profile and noses and mouths merged like those of birds, but always smaller than the birds'. By the time I was seven I was constantly drawing birds, often large pictures with pastel crayons and using different books as originals. I consumed much paper, always made quick sketches and immediately started over again on another sheet. My parents thought it would be practical to have an easel and a roll of paper, which gave me the idea to make long, pictorial stories on rolls. I was constantly sketching in the sketchbooks I was given during my growing-up years, mostly birds and nature in my surroundings but also different animals and objects that I found in other artists' pictures or even comic strips.

Man and Bird
April 1957
Pencil 37 x 50 cm (detail)

Sketchbook from 1967
Studies of Collared Flycatcher and Oak
Ink 22 x 27 cm

Landscape from Kronholmen
March 1967
34   Ink 22 x 27 cm

I made pen-and-ink drawings on glossy paper for a long period in my teens, my favourite motifs being birds and trees. The stylized branches from various defoliated trees occupied me for several years. As a child, colour crayons were important, but during a period in my teens I was in what now feels like a black-and-white phase. I often experimented by repeating the same figure time after time. The black and white illustrations came to good use in the different illustrations I made for the printed programmes of the local youth natural history group, Södertörns Fältbiologer, I belonged to. They were copied and mailed to the members.

In February 1968 I had my first real exhibition at the National Museum of Natural History in Stockholm, it was something of a break-through. After that I understood that painting birds and travel would be my destiny. The following year I travelled alone to the Faeroe Islands and had my first experiences of the Atlantic seabirds.

FÄLTBIOLOGERNA

SVERIGES FÄLTBIOLOGISKA UNGDOMSFÖRENING

Box 7234 · 103 84 Stockholm 7 · Postgiro 35 21 12

Namn

Medlemsavgiften betald

GÄLLER FÖR 1969

MEDLEMSKORT FÖR ▬ Nr 2472

Parasitic Jaeger 1970
Motif from the Faeroe Islands after a journey 1969
Oil 32 x 46 cm

The year 1972 I could devote myself to full-time painting and drawing after having finished secondary school. I contributed to six exhibitions, two of which were separate. I applied to the Academy of Arts at the beginning of the year, but was rejected which was a big disappointment to me at the time. I could, however, make a reasonable living out of my painting and travelled around Sweden bird-watching and painting.

The somewhat angular and partly stylized shapes of my seventies' paintings I see now were clearly inspired by the art of Gunnar Brusewitz (1924–2004). His style shows faint but distinct features of the art movement Constructivism which dominated the Academy in Sweden during the 1940s, at a time when he was in a similar phase of development as I was by that time. The use of geometrical pattern and rhythm are strongly influential in his style. Brusewitz became a friend and mentor after the exhibition at the Natural History Museum in Stockholm in 1968. His pictures have a perspective which is based on the human's wandering through the landscape. Sometimes he lingers over a flock of Fieldfares or a group of Goldeneyes in the ice opening, but the distance to the subject is maintained by, for example, some blades of reeds which place the observer left on the beach. The perspective is often created by a road or a path over which the birds fly, alternatively they are observed "en passant" in the middle of a field. The pictures become a summary of varying expressions during the nature walk. He called himself, tellingly, a note-taker. His technique with watercolours was clever and he was a master in conjuring a sky or a distant silhouette of a forest by minimal means. My main "Brusewitz period" was between 1970 and 1974. In 1970 a friend of my family introduced me to

the publishing company who eventually would publish my books and in this year Brusewitz' also publishes his *Skissbok (Sketchbook)*, a determining source of inspiration for me.

I spent most of the period from 1974 to 1980 painting, writing and studying birds for the series of handbooks that were to become *Fåglar i Naturen*. At the same time I was painting in both oils and watercolours for exhibitions but I felt that the development of a more independent painting style had to take second place. My watercolour technique did evolve with working on the field guides but the oilpainting suffered. In my close relation with the birds through the spotting scope during long hours of observation and sketching, a different more close up perspective evolved in my pictures. I was transferred into a nearer, more intimate space where I was with the birds and in which there were very few references at the time. Those artists who at the beginning of the century based their paintings on recently shot birds, like Fuertes and Liljefors, could often convey this proximity to subtle colour differences and fine details, the essence matter. The brothers Magnus and Vilhelm von Wright's work from the early 19th century also belongs there. I tried to develop a way to render feathers with a combination of softness and detail.

My present watercolour style was slowly formed from the mid 70s and onwards through my intensive nearness to the birds, obtained by painting directly as I saw the motif in the spotting scope. My oils from the seventies are sprawling and searching; they are comparatively few and shift from photorealism, impressionism and a style that is most similar to pointillism.

Winter landscape with Hooded Crows
Agesta 19.3.1971
Watercolour 33 x 41 cm

Chiff-Chaff in August reeds
Ågesta 31.8.1975
Watercolour 34 x 49 cm

Study of dead House Sparrow
31.8.1972
Watercolour 25 x 27 cm

Study of dead Bullfinch and Rose-hip
Käbbe, Gotland 20.10.1972
Watercolour 33 x 28 cm

My strong interest for birdplumages was early turned to Waders. During my boyhood we spent our summer holidays at a little fishing village facing a sandy bay. The shores just outside our rather tiny summer residence was teaming with migrating waders in July and August. Later, after having graduated from school in 1971, I was a free artist and I spent much time of the summers of 72 and 73 to draw waders on western Gotland. I was puzzled by the lack of adequate coverage of all the juvenile plumages that I observed – and I became aware of the need for new field guides.

At the time there was a trend in England and the U.S. with very detailed Wildlife Art, a kind of photorealism that was the trend also in the general art scene with names like Chuck Close and Gerald Richter. I did several gouache paintings of shorebirds based on a combination of my own sketches and photographs. Painting in watercolour and gouache on coloured Canson papers Robert Gillmor had taken to a master-level. I was familiar with his pictures from the covers of The Royal Society for Protection of Birds' magazine *Birds*. I had a blind from which I could see some of the less shy species very close up. Dunlins and Ruffs, especially young ones, were often unaware of my presence and came in close. The little Sandflies that sit on the mud just in front of the Ruffs enhance the proximity to the birds. Also, I had observed that the feathers of the upper back of the young

Ruffs often were lifted producing a characteristic outline, seen from a far distance, something that was unique for that species. A characteristic that I also showed on my male juvenile Ruff for the coming *Birds of Sea and Shore*. In the summer of 1973 I had a show at a gallery in Visby, the only town on the island with some of these paintings. Later the same year I was asked by a publisher to do a series of field guides based on habitats. After having submitted an outline and samples of a cover with some plates, the project took off in 1974. In September 1974 I travelled to England where the meeting with Robert Gillmor and Eric Ennion and the exhibition of Charles Tunnicliffes' *Measured drawings* at the Royal Academy made a great impact on me. The bird paintings by Leo-Paul Robert in *Les Passereaux I–III* by Paul Géroudet, which I acquired in an antiquarian bookshop in London, became my main inspiration thereafter. Brusewitz had introduced me to Robert's pictures the year before. *Louis Agassiz Fuertes & the Singular Beauty of Birds* (1971) and *Shorebirds of North America* (1968) with paintings by Robert Verity Clem were other works which also had a determining influence on me during this period. London's antiquarians with their ornithological sections were heaven for me, second only to nature, in the early 70s.

European Robin and Common Redstart 1973
Sample for *Fåglar i Naturen*
Watercolour and gouache 30 x 18 cm

Dunlins 1973
Juvenile and adult in background
Watercolour and gouache 31 x 24 cm

Juvenile Ruffs 1973
Watercolour and gouache 31 x 24 cm

Landscape from Paaviken
Gotland 6.3.1974
Watercolour 38 x 56 cm

Portrait of my brother 1977
Oil 60 x 54 cm

Self-portrait 1976
Watercolour 73 x 61 cm

41

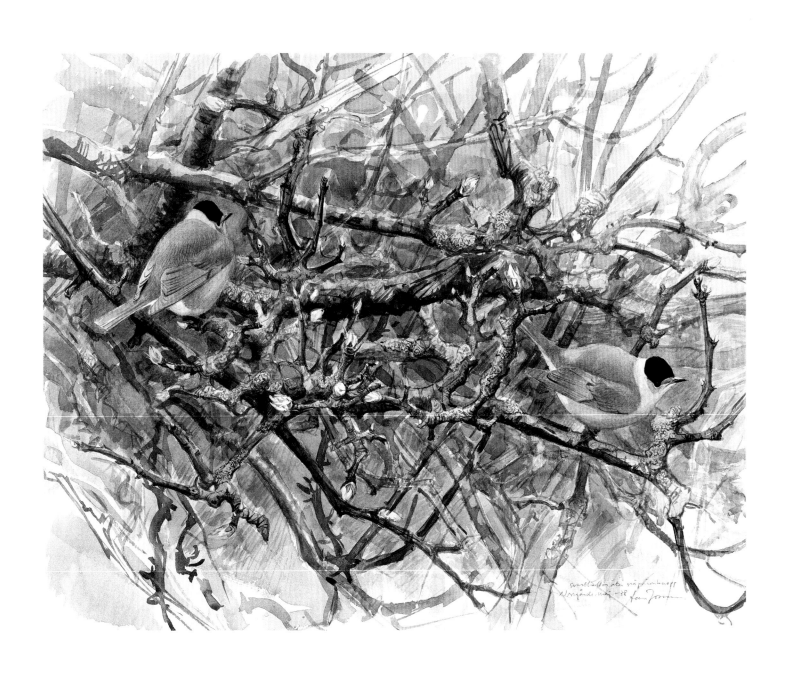

Blackcaps in Pear-tree
Norrgårde May 1978
Watercolour 48 x 60 cm

Winter Wren in winterditch
January 1980
Watercolour 46 x 31 cm

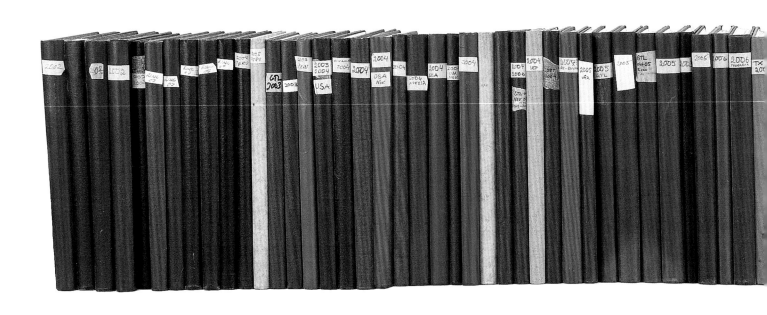

When I work in the field I almost always paint directly in front of the subject. I watch the birds in a spotting scope with between 20 and 60 times' magnification. I sketch the visual impressions with quick and direct movements on paper, actually without thinking. This is an intensive and strong way of experiencing nature for me, of both seeing and drawing. My impressions are caught in my sketchbooks, and it is from those I get inspiration when working in the studio.

My sketchbooks are bound with watercolour paper which has two different sides, one with a coarser grain and one more plain/smooth. I only use the coarser side for painting and they are bound in such a manner that they constitute a spread of one, whole sheet. I often take them out if I wish to frame and exhibit them. The measurement of the sheet is 32 x 50 cm and each page is therefore 32 x 25 cm. The books are bound by thread, but with minimal glue so the pages are easy to take apart.

Sketchbooks from 2002 – 2008
Open: Study of male Eider 2008

Sandar 4.6.07
1734

Kl. 1615 17°
10-tal dager upp här!

1820 Efter en liten paus
en skarpe vind dag
8 Myrslok. Stå med ring
men gyint. Ca 28
som det inte rörig byta
till knäspelp.
Hela flocken byter i ho
brud. dreg lite när uthärt
i tre mattre kvistar. men
ingint kun trub in med
Sanderar och Kvrlinta

Sometimes the depiction of a bird is pure, ornithological documentation like, for example, capturing the characters of an unusually patterned young gull or the moult stage of an eclipse male Common Eider. The imprints are in an equally high grade of an experience of an intensive moment at a specific time. A sketch is the visual result of seeking; it is a practice or an attempt and is therefore rarely boring. In the same way a sketch with the sole purpose of being beautiful, rarely comes alive. A sketch is a work process which rarely lies.

The spread above is taken from one of my sketchbooks, May 2007. It is a study of an arctic Ringed Plover. The species breeds on Gotland and arrives already in mid March. By the latter half of May Ringed Plovers from a different population heading towards Arctic shores sometimes stop by. They look similar, but are darker brown above and the black of the face is usually more extensive. Whilst observing these birds the local male tried to chase them off his territory, though without success. They had migrated from far away, were well fed and needed rest before embarking on the next long leg of their journey to the Arctic. They looked confident where they stood in company of some equally robust Arctic Turnstones.

Sketchbook
Studies of Red Knot
Sandar 4.6.2007 17.34 pm
Watercolour and pencil 50 x 32 cm

Study of Ringed Plover
Coast of Sindarve 23.5.2007
Watercolour and pencil 32 x 50 cm

Aurriv 14.8.2007   117

Forth tave klara duta efte eske vahndagana i klarna sava

Sketchbook
Resting Dunlin
Aurriv 14.8.2007, 11.51 am
Watercolour 32 x 50 cm

Sketchbook
Resting Commom Gull
Rivet 18.7.2006, 1 pm
Watercolour 32 x 50 cm

Ad. biane

Juv

Ad. biane

Ad. biane
Fuglai Kimslu   17.07
Sudane   13.7.07

Toipipu

In the field I observe and start the drawing within six to eight seconds. That is the length of the human's short visual memory; it is the time within which the picture is still on the retina. If I lose a detail, like an outline or a hue over the breast, in the midst of sketching or painting, I do not rely on previous experience but observe my model again to rediscover it. I do not have a photographic memory, but a trained ability to draw what I actually see. I do not repeat those pictures that already are imprinted in my memory as I draw what I actually see and that in its turn adds new experience. It is not unusual for me to feel like a medium that catches the moment or the presence of the individual bird in a defined space or specific time. The imprint is partly independent from previous images or experiences. Each plover is a new plover, each eider is observed as if it was the first. If the bird disappears, the sketch is halted, that is where the excitement is. In practice I often have to complete or continue an on-going watercolour after the motif has flown away. The underlying drawing, the fact that I have carefully observed and drawn a specific detail, will be the key to my memory. It will draw forth the image anew.

It is often a question of taking advantage of the moment. These Red-backed Shrikes had been breeding just outside the studio, and I knew the family would hang around for a while. It would take a few more days before they would all start their autumn migration to tropical Africa.

Studies of Red-backed Shrikes
Sindarve 13.8.2007

Male, juvenile and bill of adult female
Pencil and watercolour 32 x 50 cm

Juvenile, head of adult female and Whitethroat
5.09 pm
Pencil and watercolour 32 x 50 cm

Juvenile Red-backed Shrike
Watercolour 32 x 25 cm (detail)

Study of Apple and Hawthorn blossom, drawing of Barred Warbler
Sundre 30.5.2008, 12.35 am
Watercolour and pencil 32 x 50 cm

Singing Red-backed Shrike in Hawthorn
Sundre 30.5.2008, 1.22 pm
Watercolour and pencil 32 x 25 cm

Wood Sandpipers are often active when migrating, constantly busy foraging, which makes defining details difficult. This bird stood completely still on a rock and showed her feet well, also unusual for a bird that usually hides them in mud and swampy meadows. I found this individual in fresh spring plumage at Faludden, just a few kilometres from my studio. I was surprised when I found it still there the next day, which gave me an opportunity to add some more detail to my sketch. The most thrilling challenge was to reveal its face and its special facial expressions. I found it showed a weak angle on the ridge of the bill, which I had not seen before, enhanced by a light grey wedge. Perhaps it was specific for this particular individual.

Wood Sandpiper and Greenshank belong to the genus *Tringa* which often have a leg colour that has given them their specific names. The Wood Sandpiper has a beautiful warm avocado-green colour to its legs while the much larger Greenschank has a cold grey-green tone. Their plumage is ,however, mostly grey and especially drab when they return from their northern breeding grounds in July. In May, however, the Wood Sandpiper often look very handsome with pearl white spots on the dark scapulars. Both species breed on the vast bogs in the north and migrate past Gotland. The Spring migration is concentrated to the first week of May and they start to return back early, already from the third week of June. Young birds leave their breeding grounds later and they start to turn up in mid July and can be seen all through August.

Study of Wood Sandpiper
Faludden 7–8.5.2007
Pencil and watercolour 32 x 50 cm

Study of Greenschank
Coast of Sindarve 2.5.2007
Watercolour 50 x 32 cm

Greenshank
18.01 Finlake coast
Trooping calmly for an hour. Resting mostly a few minute

Bill lacks any colour here,
basically neutral grey. Legs dull greengrey
In the sun quite light and with a stroke of
warmth.

Redbene
'tulu (lut) 'tulu lut 'tulu let
malande

Saw { kullie kullie kullie ....
       köll köll köll

Study of the brother

Sketchbook
Study of juvenile Peregrine Falcon
25.9.2004
Pencil and watercolour 2 pages 32 x 25 cm

As a young bird-watcher in the 60s and 70s the Peregrine Falcon was a rarity, badly hit by the mercury used in the seed for sowing. The first bird I ever saw on Gotland was a young individual in October 1980. A bird I still remember as it was the first wild Peregrine I ever drew and painted in the field. The recovery of the Peregrine population has been amazing and nowadays it is a regular visitor to my area. The same feeling of excitement and eagerness still comes over me at the sighting of a large falcon, of any species. Their presence usually stir the local birds up and they seem to rule any place where they turn up. The bird above, a young female, had just finished her bath and was drying her wings. It had company of what I regarded as her brother, they often performed in the air together and at one point they took flight and chased another Peregrine away that passed overhead. A few minutes after I had finished my study she caught up with a Starling, and gracefully and without any effort picked it out of the air, as a ripe fruit from a tree.

Study of adult Peregrine Falcon
Skagit flats, Washington 9.11.2006, 12.00–1.30 pm
Watercolour 32 x 25 cm

1976

Holmer vatten

Hanne trurn dag hun
har ställe i ett ängsmis int
då nätte timme igte lite
og sammtal per sammlum

Avanes Holmer vatten
11.5.06

September 2003
1:a skiss i på Höj föres
Äste i varben

11 Maj 2006
Dalm ... 1833-2005

An unusually expressive Lapwing and her chicks kept me captivated a few days in May. I sat in my Volkswagen van and the chicks were sometimes only a few metres from my car. The days were sunny and orchids and meadow saxifrages had begun to straighten up after slow growth due to a couple of days with cold nights. I cannot put into words how much I appreciated having the opportunity to follow a family of waders like this for a few days. I saw how they had grown during the night and encountered dangers their parents warned against, such as a Raven or a Herring Gull that passed over. They walk systematically all over the territory when foraging. The first days huddling under the warm mother, but as the days went by they became more and more independent. Each chick had its individual expression and in this situation I often find a particular one that becomes my favourite. They are in constant movement, and it is difficult to capture their special expression.

Study of Lapwing with chicks

Holmar 11.5.2006, 7.16 pm
Pencil and watercolour 32 x 50 cm

Holmar 11.5.2006, 6.37 – 8.15 pm
Pencil and watercolour 32 x 50 cm

Lapwing chick and Green-winged Orchid
17.5.2006, 10.28 am
Watercolour 32 x 50 cm

22·4·07·

The reason why females have a lighter, brown area below eye and some creamy or golden in their neckstripe. Resting in the mossy meadows.

22.4.07
The reason why females have a lighter brown
area below the eye and some creamy or golden in
their neckstripe. Resting on the mossy meadows.

During most of one day I followed a young Ringed Plover, almost fully grown. It stayed within a limited area of perhaps 50 square metres, where it rested, preened or fed. Both parents were nearby and kept watchful eyes from a limestone outcrop that emerged from the flat ground. The juvenile often rested on or next to the rock which was covered in mosses and White and Golden Stonecrop. Yellow Rattle and Kidney Vetch flowered in the surrounding meadow. The dark markings of the bird created interesting compositions and I saw an interesting motif in the bird's special expression and the round shapes of the fossils and mosses of the stone.

Young Ringed Plover and Yellow Rattle
Hamra 25.6.2006, 10.25 am
Pencil and watercolour 32 x 50 cm

European Golden Plover
22.4.2007
Watercolour 25 x 32 cm

Young Ringed Plover and Stonecrop
Hamra 25.6.2006, 4.37 pm
Pencil and watercolour 32 x 50 cm

The Baltic island of Gotland, with its limestone-rich soil, is a haven for orchids. I have painted more plants in recent years than ever before, even if vegetation has always been an important component in my bird art. Some say that ornithologists become interested in flowers when their eyesight starts failing, and I must admit that thanks to my more frequent use of glasses I have been able to study flowers in greater detail again. I always lie down when painting plants as the ground level perspective is important. Neighbouring plants and various insects are often incorporated to give a holistic image of the plant and its environment. There are 28 species of orchids on the island.

Elder-flowered Orchid, Burnt Orchid and Sheep Fescue
Valar 1.5.2005, 4.45 and 5.20 pm
Pencil and watercolour 32 x 50 cm

Sketchbook
Early Marsh Orchid, Willowleaf Yellowhead and Flesh-fly
Vamlingbo 4.6.2007
Watercolour and pencil 32 x 50 cm

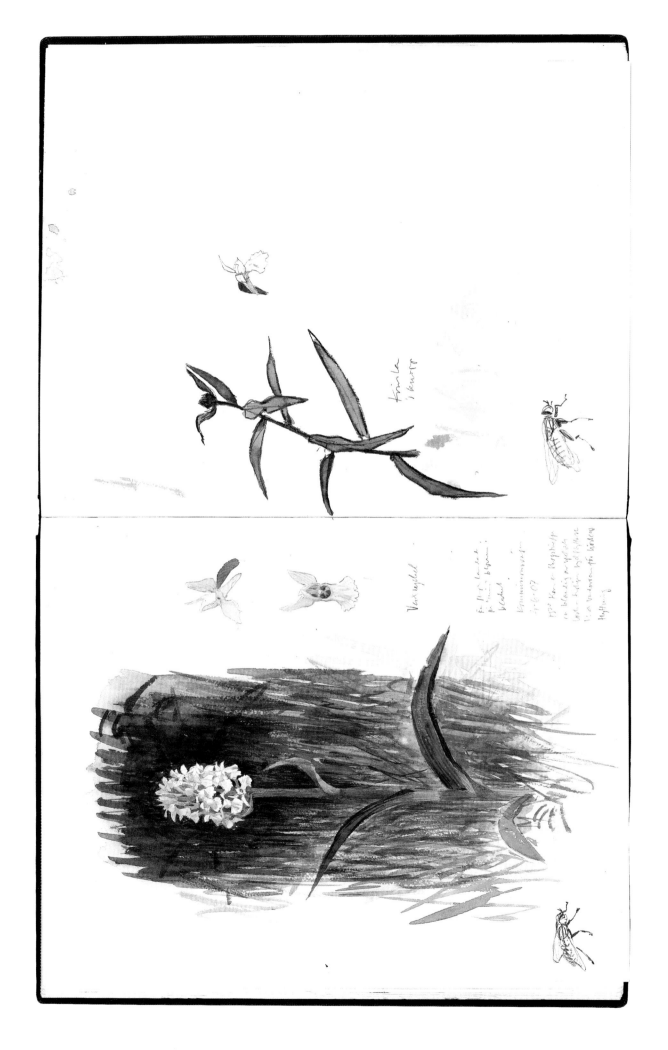

Road 16's 287 1271

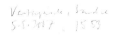

Verbascum Studie
5·5·2017 · 15.53

Primrose
Rivet 15.5.2007, 12.37 pm
Watercolour 32 x 50 cm

Small Pasque Flower
Sundre 5.5.2007, 3.53 pm
Watercolour 32 x 50 cm

Spring Pheasant's eye
Kettelvik 18.4.2004
Watercolour 25 x 32 cm

WATERCOLOURS

The watercolour often has immediacy as the water, or colour pigments on the wet sheet, lives its own life. It undergoes transformation while I return my eye to the eyepiece to study my motif. I am the link between two realities in constant change, just like the narrow passage sand has to pass through between the two cones of an hourglass. I often have the experience of disappearing, dissolving into the sketch or outdoor watercolour painting. The friction between eye and hand can suddenly disappear and it is more the feeling rather than the intellect that is the fibre cable that runs between eye lens and brush.

The Sun is About to Set
Eiders
Rivet 29.4.2008, 8.18 pm
Watercolour 56 x 76 cm

Returning with a Strong South-wester
Rivet 12.3.2007
Watercolour 30 x 42 cm

After the Winterstorm
Rivet 25.2.2008, 12.20 pm
Watercolour 56 x 76 cm

69

Wintermale Eider
Rivet 28.1.2008
Watercolour 45 x 56 cm

Winterfemale Eider
Rivet 28.1.2008
Watercolour 34 x 56 cm

Wings that Come to Rest
Common Eiders, Rivet 17.4.2008
Watercolour 56 x 76 cm

The Common Eider has always fascinated me as a subject. They are large, powerful ducks with a sculptural silhouette and both sexes present different artistic challenges. The male is faceless as his eye disappears in the black crown, his shape and plumage create different abstract patterns depending on the angle of observation and what he is up to. The unusual greenish hue in his flow of "hair" has a mystical quality to it which seems impossible to do justice in a watercolour; it has the character of marzipan which is caused by both feather structure and colour hue. The rest of the body appears white from a distance but shows subtle tones of pink and lemon-yellow which shift with individual and light. The belly is a velvety black but reflects the temperature of the sun's rays. The female, on the other hand, has eyes resembling currants, which radiate good-naturedness, like a fairy tale godmother. Her facial expression often reinforces the picture; if her charisma is wrong everything collapses. The shapes of the different feather layers and tracts are accentuated by the evenly darkly barred individual feathers. While the white parts of the male reflect all the bluish hues of the sky, these hues are completely absorbed by the deeply dormant grey, beige and reddish-brown tones of the female. They reflect the sea as a living environment.

The two water colours to the right are painted on the same day and the titles allude to an experiment to apply blue on the wet, yellowish basic tone, or, alternatively, yellow on a bluish tone. The colour tones of the underwater plants are refracted through the waves which function as prisms; the even surfaces reflect the sky, optical illusions, the magic of water.

A Fresh South-wester
Eiders, Aurriv 4.5.2007, 9.50 am
Watercolour 56 x 76 cm

Blue in Yellow
Eiders, Aurriv 21.5.2002
Watercolour 53 x 76 cm

Yellow in Blue
Eiders, Aurriv 22.5.2002
Watercolour 56 x 76 cm

Waves of Colour 2007
Common Gulls
Watercolour 61 x 76 cm

A Warm Evening 2003
Common Gulls
Rivet 11.8.2003
Watercolour 57 x 76 cm

Against All Winds 2002
Great Black-backed Gulls
Watercolour 75 x 106 cm

The Whiteness 2007
Young Herring Gull
Watercolour 57 x 76 cm

Down at the southernmost point of Gotland there is a reef. It extends a few hundred metres in a south-western direction, and is called Rivsuddden or Rivet, which I often write as a location on my watercolours.

A varying number of stones, depending on the water depth, break the water. The Baltic Sea does not experience tides but the air pressure produces a difference in depth of normally plus or minus 20 centimetres. The stones, of gneiss and granite of different minerals, are often polished and rounded by the sea's movements and have been transported here by the latest glaciation. The local stone is sandstone and reef limestone which form pale slabs. These rocks are platforms on which the living sculptures of gulls, mergansers and cormorants can rest on, it is like a park of sculptures. There is always a gallery of models present, models that are a never-ending source of inspiration. The wind from the south-west predominates and the perspective from land is often from behind and to the side as they face the wind. With the help of my telescope I move myself into their world, capture their characters, expressions and temporary spatial atmospheres.

Clear Water 2004
Lesser Black-backed Gulls
Watercolour 57 x 76 cm

Sleeping Form 2002
Redbreasted Merganser
Watercolour 57 x 76 cm

Sunflooded 2002
Eurasian Wigeons
Watercolour 53 x 75 cm

Light 2002
Pied Avocets
Watercolour 49 x 62 cm

Stockvike is, together with Rivet, my most important workplace. From a headland called Aurriv I can get a complete view of a shallow sandy bay which is rich in birds all year round. Open, grazed littoral meadows surround it and harbour eleven species of breeding waders, not counting Woodcock which breeds in the adjacent forests. Another 20 species of waders are regular on migration and I have encountered 14 vagrant wader species during the 30 years I have lived here. Eurasian Curlew and Pied Avocet are both common breeders and I closely monitor their annual life cycles from March when they arrive until the last ones leave the island in autumn. The female curlews with their long bills are attracted to the shores of the bay and its bristleworms, while the males guide the young over the vast grassy meadows in pursuit of insects. The adults have altogether left us after the 1st of July and the migration peaks around midsummer, even if single birds pass all summer. Many young birds from breeding areas far to the north-east pass us in August and a small group has lingered in recent years and tried to overwinter. This is a new feature, but they are often forced further south by the midwinter cold. I rarely saw avocets after July before, but in recent years they have stayed on until September.

Longing 2006
Eurasian Curlew
Watercolour 43 x 76 cm

Linnet Country
Hamra 23.4.2007
Watercolour 25 x 32 cm

Marsh at Aurriv 2006
Watercolour 38 x 57 cm

The short-sward coastal meadows become waterlogged in winter and many depressions retain the water until spring. These small, wet mires are focal points for waders' activities. The Redshank with its young are attracted here in the early summer and most waders visit their own mire for bathing, preening and foraging between the shifts on the nest. The Garganeys and Shovelers come here in pairs, using the mires as starting points for their excursions in the landscape to choose a suitable breeding location. A grassy hillock which has grown up next to a rock becomes the nesting site for the local pair of Common Gulls or a vantage point for an Arctic Tern on the lookout. Spotted Redshanks and Greenshanks take a rest here on their way to a remote bog in Lapland. I can sit here for hours just observing the life which unfolds and enacts before me. Time is often crucial, the newly hatched redshank chicks rarely make themselves known until after an hour or so when they feel safe and secure enough. I myself use my VW bus as a hide from where to follow the happenings. Perhaps I am more concealed from the world than from the birds? They continuously watch and react on every movement. Perhaps it is my identity as a human being that is hidden, maybe that is why I am so at home in this place.

Worrying Times
Redschank with chicks, Aurriv 31.5.2004
Watercolour 38 x 57 cm

Male Garganey
Aurriv 1.6.2004
Watercolour 32 x 25 cm

Resting Garganey 2007
7.37 pm
Watercolour 32 x 25 cm

Garganey pair 2006
Aurriv 1.6.2004
Watercolour 39 x 52 cm

No Light
Eurasian Teal 2.11.2007, 6 pm
Watercolour 29 x 39 cm

Condensed
Eurasian Teal 23.9.2007
Watercolour 39 x 53 cm

88

E urasian Teals became the centre of my attention in autumn 2007. The stage was the inner part of Stockvike where they make a long stopover during their southward migration. I had focussed on ducks, dabbling ducks in particular, for some time and teals were common and could be approached. In autumn they moult into their display, or winter, dress and I could follow a few individuals from one week to another. The characteristic which is last acquired as winter plumage is the black line along the side of the back (outer scapulars) and on the female the feathers on the edge of the belly's flanks are the last to be replaced. The days were clear towards the end of October and November. The sun set early and I was usually still sitting there until darkness fell. A couple of magical sunsets in November caused the light to play over the bay as if in a dreamworld . After a couple of hours of conditions as these, a marvellous, final light would creep in and I painted frantically in my attempts to capture it. It reminded me of a solar eclipse, over so quickly I was left wondering if it had really happened at all. Within me I was reflecting that nobody had ever written about November sunsets, especially not starring teals. It could actually be worth a mass, the experience was spiritual for me.

In the Land of the Teals
October 2007
Watercolour 57 x 76 cm

Pintails are often shy birds in northern Europe and I rarely get really close to them. I visited the nature reserve Bosque del Apache in southern New Mexico in November 2004. Huge numbers of wildfowl and cranes rest and spend the winter there. My hopes were set on experiencing some crisp late-autumn days but it turned into a week of rain which eventually transformed into snow. Everything was well organised and accessible, as is often the case in U.S. reserves, and I drove around comfortably in my car on the road banks encompassing the wetlands. Protected from the weather inside my car I used my telescope through the window and arranged my rain gear to prevent snow from whirling into the car. I had many hours of trepid contemplation over the huddled nature of Pintails sitting amongst water plants and snow. I discovered an optical phenomenon in these sessions of detailed study; the water drops formed by melting snow on the birds' breast feathers. The large drops reflected the dark water on the inside of the drops' upper side, and the paler sky was reflected in the bottom of the drop. The dark grey tones of the mantle were reflected in the same way in the water drops on the shoulder. These are small details, often unnoticed, appearing when one has visually followed a male that slowly revolves on his axis, cowering in his soft grey plumage.

Study of female Pintail
Bombay Hook, Delaware 2.11.2006
Watercolour 45 x 42 cm

detail

Resting in Grey
Pintail 13.11.2004
Watercolour 29 x 37 cm

Study of resting Pintail
Bosque del Apache, New Mexico 13.11.2004
Watercolour 32 x 25 cm

Tired Crow
Hooded Crow
Rivet 24.5.2005, 9.43 am
Watercolour 25 x 32 cm

When Will Something Happen
Rook, Hoburgen 24.4.2004
Watercolour 28 x 40 cm

Balance 2006
Common Buzzard
Watercolour 57 x 76 cm

93

Cold Winds 2003
Golden Eagle
Watercolour 57 x 76 cm

Study of a young Golden Eagle
20.10.2005
Watercolour 32 x 25 cm (detail)

Study of a young Golden Eagle
29.4.2006
Watercolour 32 x 50 cm (detail)

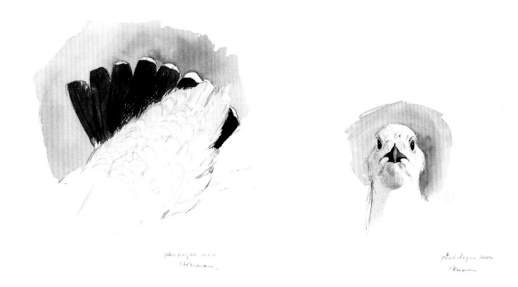

Tailstudy of a Willow Grouse
Hemvan, Lappland 2004
Watercolour 32 x 25 cm (detail)

Portrait of a Willow Grouse
Hemavan, Lappland 2004
Watercolour 32 x 25 cm (detail)

Willow Grouse in Mountain Birch 2004
Watercolour 31 x 56 cm

Golden Eagle in Snow
Sundre 6.2.2003
Watercolour 51 x 36 cm

Winter Patterns 2008
Gyrfalcon
Watercolour 57 x 76 cm

Mountain Storm 2004
Ptarmigans
Watercolour 45 x 68 cm

Kanin, Russia
12.6.1994
Watercolour 34 x 56 cm

Kolguyev, Russia
14.6.1994, 1.45 pm
Watercolour 34 x 56 cm

I have had a strong craving for Arctic Siberia since the days of my youth; the land from which migrating Curlew Sandpipers and Grey Plovers come from during late summer days, the land to which are destined thousands of Barnacle Geese in mid May. This dream was fulfilled in 1991 when I was able to travel to Arctic Siberia with a group of British ornithologists. In 1994, I joined an expedition along the North-east passage on board the ship Academic Feodorov with a group of Swedish and Russian scientists. We were brought ashore by helicopter to many places on the north Siberian tundra. The landscape, with its endless horizons, may be perceived as one of frightening grandeur by many but it made a deep impression on me. I painted and studied birds, mammals, plants and insects intensively during that busy summer.

In 2003, I had the opportunity to board another vessel travelling along the Kuril Islands, Kamchatka, the Aleutian Islands and the Islands of the Bering Strait. It added the last leg in the completion of a north-east passage from Scandinavia to Japan via the Arctic Ocean.

Gyrfalcon
Nome, Alaska 15.6.2003
Watercolour 57 x 76 cm

Yamal, Russia
19.6.1994, 11.40 am
Watercolour 25 x 32 cm

The Islands of Dark Fulmars
2007
The Kuril Islands, Russia
Watercolour 76 x 106 cm

Page 104

Western Sandpiper
St. Lawrence Island, Alaska, May 2003
Watercolour 24 x 32 cm

Red-necked Stint
Hokkaido, Japan 22.5.2003, 1 pm
Watercolour 32 x 25 cm (detail)

Zhupanovo River, Kamchatka, Russia
5.6.2003
Watercolour 28 x 38 cm

Ostrova Biel Chirpyev
The Kuril Islands, Russia
31.5.2003
Watercolour 24 x 32 cm

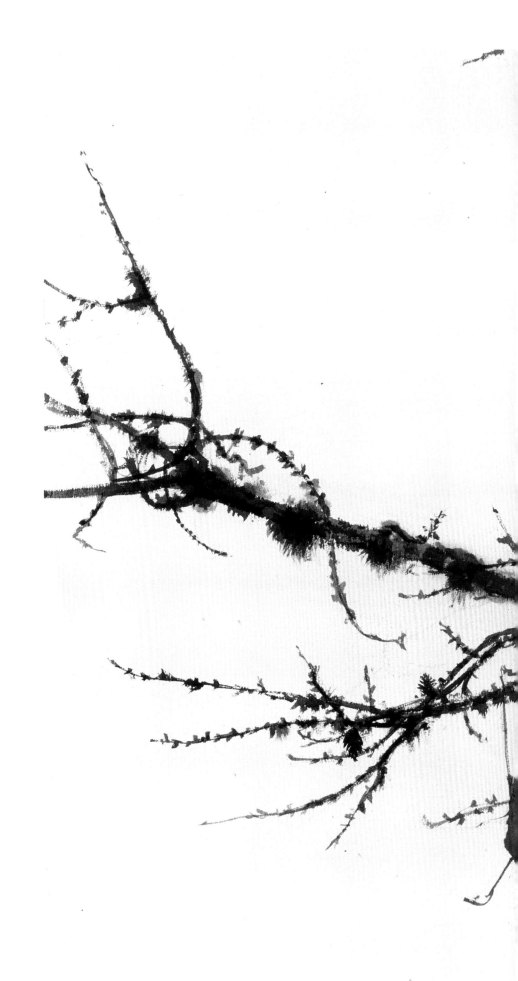

The Owl at Ovalon 1991
Great Grey Owl
Watercolour 97 x 110 cm

November Apples 1992
Eurasian Magpie
Watercolour 45 x 68 cm

Female Bullfinches and dry Ash-fruits
Norrgårde 10.2.1991
Watercolour 40 x 34 cm

Suddenly and totally unexpected it sat there; a Long-eared Owl in the top of a juniper. Right next to the brown shed where the school bus stops, by our road turn-off. I was heading back for lunch, without my binoculars or drawing kit. I looked at the bird for a few minutes, and then went to my studio to get the telescope and sketchbook. The bird was cooperating and was still there when I returned and I could draw it from close range. It was mostly huddled together with its eyes half-closed, but occasionally it stretched its neck and scrutinised the snow-covered ground with great attention as if it had heard something. Long-eared Owls are nocturnal and are rarely found in the open like this in the middle of the day. The snow was falling slowly, with heavy, white flakes towards a backdrop of young pines. A Christmas card in Advent.

Sketchbook 2003
Studies of Long-eared Owl
Pencil 32 x 50 cm

Something of interest 2004
Long-eared Owl
Watercolour 56 x 50 cm

Pygmy Shrew

Young female Blackbird and Rose-hips
Common Blackbird 2004
Watercolour 28 x 33 cm

Study of Barn Owl
13.12.2006
Watercolour 43 x 52 cm

Study of female Greenfinch
Sindarve 7.10.2007
Watercolour 32 x 25 cm

Through the Air 2004
Eurasian Sparrowhawk and Greenfinch
Watercolour 57 x 76 cm

Study of incubating Eurasian Woodcock
Skoge, Sundre, 8.5.2007, 9 am–1.35 pm
Watercolour 50 x 32 cm

Hepatica 2004
Kettelvik 19.4.2004, 11.30 am
Watercolour 32 x 25 cm

116

Woodcocks are common in the forests where I live. I see them during spring and early summer evenings when they fly in display against the evening sky and forest. It is not too unusual that I flush them in the forest, but then they are reddish-brown shadows escaping with quick wingbeats in among the trunks and branches. The best chance of seeing one is while driving around at night in the landscape during the summer or late autumn when they are often perched on the tarmac roads, but the headlights do not do their plumage justice. I was tipped off, or rather guided to, the bird on the opposite page which lay by a stone fence in a pasture overgrown by hazel and birch. I did not see her blink once during the hours I painted her, she was absolutely still and I suffered a bad conscience for subjecting her to this uncomfortable process. She probably blinked when I looked down into my sketchbook. On one occasion I went back to the car to get some more water, and she then took the opportunity to move a little. She was outstanding as a subject, completely still during four and a half hours. Even the shiny yellow Buttercup in front of her moved faster as it strived to follow the sun which wandered slowly across the mid-morning sky. Several bird species that brood quietly on the forest floor and press hard to the ground when an enemy approaches have developed a cryptic camouflage. The hen Black Grouse, the hen Capercaillie, the Nightjar and the Woodcock appear exquisitely beautiful and sophisticated, painted by evolution as illusory fragments of forest. The dry, brownish-red oak leaves, the mouldering aspen leaves, the sticks from deciduous trees, thin as little fingers, and the black-spotted fragments of bark can all be read in the intricate plumage patterns and colour tones of the Woodcock. If I was to choose one object that could convey the whole nature of the forest to creatures on another planet, it would be a Woodcock. He who gazes into her eye and interprets her mottled cowl will instinctively understand what a northern forest in spring is about.

Spring Evening 1998
View from the studio
Watercolour 24 x 32 cm

The Spirit of the Woods 2008
Eurasian Woodcock
Watercolour 62 x 75 cm

Holmar 27.4.2007, 9.13 am

Identify a place, one hundred square metres of littoral meadow, a cairn, a dried-out ditch, a row of fence posts along the road. White Wagtail and Northern Wheatear will be sharing territory for 2–3 months. The wheatear, a first year male, flies in and out of the cairn; checks the nest site and chases midgets, lands on the meadow among daisies and ribwort – a Skylark crosses the road, curlew and lark are singing
Suddenly, they are gone. Is the female laying? Has the male found a better feeding place? Or both? Has the site not blossomed yet nor reached its peak in insect abundance? Is there a marsh or pasture nearby that attracts? I wait for their return.

9.23 am, returned. He (the wagtail) is suddenly perched on the cairn and "sli-witts" – it seems like he has emerged from the world of stones – but soon flies undulating away over the fields where the Barnacle Geese usually graze. He perches on a fencepost, – gazes 80–110 metres away – flies back and settles on the field closest to the cairn. Then the female appears from the stones and flies over the field. He follows – they apparently forage there together, or are they looking for another nesting site?

I followed them, to a pile of earth with organic refuse from my neighbour's farm; this was more nourishing and presumably attracted more insects.

Sketchbook
Study of White Wagtail
Holmar 27.4.2008, 9.30 am
Watercolour 25 x 32 cm

White Wagtail in winter plumage
Aurriv 22.8.2007, 5.21 pm
Watercolour 25 x 32 cm

Page 121

The Wagtail 1988
White Wagtail
Watercolour 50 x 40 cm

In Evening Dress 2006
Common Shelducks
Olja 73 x 100 cm

Under Protection 1999
Eurasian Oystercatcher with chicks
Oil 60 x 81 cm

Before the Night 2000
Caspian Terns
Oil 80 x 120 cm

Following pages

Evening Curlews 2008
Eurasian Curlews
Oil 110 x 180 cm

Expression 2002
Northern Lapwing
Oil 73 x 100 cm

In Turqouise 2002
Pied Avocets
Oil 61 x 80 cm

Following pages

Patterns of Tranquillity 2007
Pintails
Oil 110 x 180 cm

Rest 2001
Pied Avocets
Oil 73 x 100 cm

Thoughts on a Grey Day 2006
Common Gulls
Oil 81 x 100 cm

133

When painting this bird, at close range in the car through my spotting scope, I was initially fully fixated on capturing the head and shape of the face by modulating the white through colours and light. The variations in shade are subtle, but so substantial and change with the small movements the bird makes. Standing head-on into the wind, the head is never still; it turns back and forth in a roughly 30° angle; small twists which are repeated with what seems to be regular intervals. As one has started to paint the face at a certain angle, one must often wait until the next time the face comes into the same position though perhaps slightly displaced. It is the fine colours of the shaded parts that form the head and produce the shape of the face, everything is basically white with tiny variations, which makes the evaluation very subtle. I think it took me twenty minutes to modulate the white to create the Gulls head. When I inserted the black eye everything became dislocated again, and I felt disappointed. The steel-grey mantle etched itself onto the retina beside the macula lutea and when the bird took off and vanished I had to paint it referring to my memory and therefore I used the word "dared" in my notes below. When it returned 20 minutes later, I saw a more reddish hue in the grey, but I was uncertain if it was my memory that failed me or the light that had changed. I commented on the painting:

Dared paint the mantle. After having focussed on looking in the face for thirty minutes, I felt that the mantle hues had etched themselves into my memory – it took 20 minutes until she returned, leaning slightly forwards, and I then felt that the tones were more red, grey-mauve (against). Changed, but thought that maybe the angle or light had changed, did however see pale edgings to the scapulars, which I scratched in.
When it started to rain and I was studying the greater coverts, I saw something brown in the tone, a touch of burnt umber. It was the male of the pair, not the female. She had a fine rosy touch to the belly and breast but had an injury to the right leg which she did not want to rest on.

6 pm finished.
The birds were gone.
16.4 08.

The painting of a Common Gull on the opposite page, which stands alone in a large body of water and surf, is made on the southernmost promontory of Gotland, Rivet. The top image shows the painting after I came home, i.e. those parts that have been created outdoors on site. The lower image shows the final result. It is important for me to capture the "sense of light" itself. Each opportunity has a specific and unique light which makes up much of the picture's content and reflects my mood of the moment, which for some reason is important to retain, like the moment of writing a poem; if it is edited too much it dies. It can become something else, maybe as beautiful, maybe better, but it can never convey the actual experience at the time. An edited diary is readable, but can never replace words that were written in the actual moment.

Study of a Common Gull 2008
Oil 46 x 61 cm

By the Sea 2004
Common Gull
Oil 83 x 92 cm

135

Yesterday I sat all day in my VW bus and painted in oils down by the southernmost promontory, Rivet. The air was stirred by a fresh wind from the south-west, humid and grey but mild. Grey weather is perfect for painting in oils; the light is contained without shadows or colour temperatures changing too quickly. It is a ritual to stock the bus with all the gear and paraphernalia when leaving for oil painting, one never knows if it will work out or not. But everything was perfect and distinctly inspiring; gulls of different sizes crouching in the wind and their whiteness against pale grey water and dark green umber or lead grey waves. I felt a bit out of practise, having mostly painted in watercolours for a while. I was squatting in my old, worn-out, office chair which had replaced one of the seats in the bus, with a canvas and all the requisite equipment that filled up the whole car. Many Common Gulls, single Herring Gulls, three old and one juvenile Great Black-backed Gull sat among the first row of stones. After I had drawn a Great Black-backed Gull in some detail, a young White-tailed Eagle flew into the scene and spooked the gulls and cormorants which took flight. I quickly grabbed all my watercolour paraphernalia and contrived to sketch the large, ruffled eagle perched on a rock on a large watercolour paper in 20 minutes or so without thinking. What a creature! When it flew off, the charcoal drawing of the Great Black-backed Gull appeared lifeless. I looked around and soon found a new gull that aroused my interest for painting. I painted one bird standing, found another lying, and placed them both on the same rock which I saw further out against the surf. Then I sat, for six hours, painting while the light changed from the compact, grey morning light to a hazy afternoon sun. When one is sitting and trying to determine which white colour a white-headed gull under a compact cloud covers should have, the result is still just white, maybe with a faint nuance of green or mauve. As the sunlight slowly appears, it feels as if the white becomes whiter, twice as white, but still there is only the same zinc-white paint tub to use, although one wishes for a "double white". The shadows can always be made darker but then the water of my painting was already dark as under a lead-grey sky. Later, in the studio, I found the painting lacked something; it missed elements that felt lost. I struggled hard to recreate the atmosphere I had experienced, but it became more and more of a re-construction. I removed the lying bird and replaced it with a young bird next to it, brought in from one of my sketches. Finally, it became not more than a half-completed image.

This morning, when I saw the picture again, I decided to return to the same spot with the same canvas and try again. A clear sense of presence was missing. As I drove the 15 minutes or so it takes to reach Rivet and Hoburgen, the rain increased and my expectations diminished. The gulls were still there when I arrived and despite visibility being worse than the previous day I even recognised yesterday's Great Black-backed Gull. I tried to re-establish the almost greyish-brown hues that the rain brought to the water from

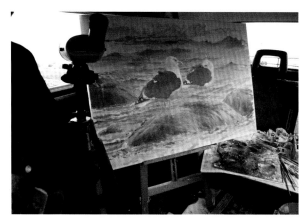

In my Studio bus

Study of a young White-tailed Eagle
Rivet 16.10.07
Watercolour 57 x 76 cm

At the end of the day

the initial feeling of yesterday, but which I had successively changed into cold grey and greenish-blue tones during the evening session in the studio. I was once more captivated by the motif and changed the rock, the water and exchanged the sub-adult with a second adult gull standing in the same direction, against the wind. The way all Gulls rest when the wind is blowing.

To sit and directly observe the motif through a spotting scope, and mix the different shades of oil colour to delineate material and the light's sculpting of the gulls is magical for me. The feeling of daring, of insisting and letting the subtle colours create the feeling of rock, wind, water and feathers is a strong experience. Time runs by and there is always the feeling of never having enough time; that the strokes have to be forced, the characteristics simplified. But to me this is a positive experience. The rain leaked persistently into the van but the greyish tones accumulated on the canvas. I was pleased with my day. The grey, rainy 17th of October, 2007.

Following pages

Living with the Wind 2007
Great Black-backed Gulls
Oil 80 x 120 cm

Against the Wind 2006
Common Gulls
Oil 60 x 81 cm

Aproaching Storm 1999
Common Eiders
Oil 80 x 120 cm

Following pages

Wings Over the Kars Sea 2007
King Eiders
Oil 110 x 180 cm

141

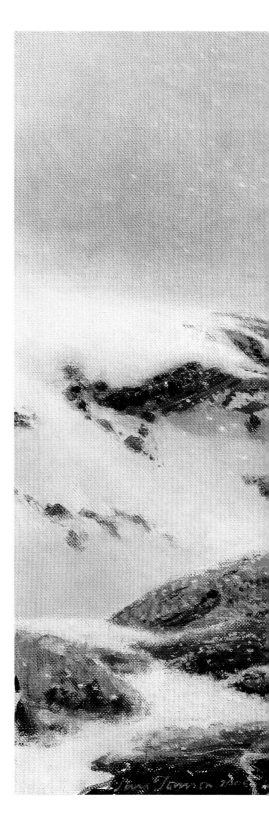

The study above is from the skin collection at the Zoological Museum in Copenhagen, Denmark. There are a large number of Greenland falcons, i.e. Gyrfalcons from Greenland, in it. Many of the specimens were prepared by the medical doctor and ornithologist Theodor N. Krabbe who collected all killed Gyrfalcons which were awarded premiums at the turn of the 19th century. Krabbe was one of the first to warn about the effects of the unrestrained hunting that took place on Greenland during these days. I have mixed emotions when I study these beautiful falcons; for me as an artist they are a delightful sight, the variation in their plumages, each one more beautiful than the other. They vary in colouration from almost purely dark-grey to pristine white and between the two extremes there is an unlimited array of intricate patterns built up by bands, tear-shaped drops and spatters of pepper. The birder in me feels sadness. The oil is inspired by one of these birds which ceased to live as young and wild a long time ago. The perhaps three-month old female met its destiny on August 26, 1948, in Pearyland, in the northernmost part of Greenland which Knud Rasmussen and Peter Freuchen, on their dramatic first Thule Expedition in 1912, established as a part of Greenland. I have not been to Greenland myself; the background to my Greenland Falcons is inspired by less dramatic excursions. The cliff lies next to a lift called "Kungsliften" in the Swedish Tärna fjells in Lapland. I usually leave the piste and post myself with a camera and sketchbook to study Ptarmigan among the stone blocks. If it gets cold I strap on the skis and find myself in the café within five minutes, enjoying a hot chocolate – things were definitely different in Knud Rasmussen's time.

Studies of Greenland Gyrfalcons 2004
Zoologisk Museum, Copenhagen
Pencil 32 x 50 cm

Young and Wild 2005
Gyrfalcon
Oil 73 x 100 cm

144

The First Dawn 2005
White Gyrfalcons
Oil 80 x 120 cm

November Snow 2007
Eurasian Magpies
Oil 81 x 100 cm

Hooded Crows are always available as motifs; on the fields, by the beach and outside my studio window. I was yearning to continue painting directly from a model after having completed November Snow, but the snow had melted away. A couple of crows were perched in the top of one of the trees in my small copse and I started to paint the middle bird through my telescope, through the triple-glazed windows, more as a study. It soon flew away and I started with another one. The two left birds had, for the most part, acquired their shape after that session. The following day I noticed that the painting needed some more weight to the right, so I made the right bird from an older sketch I had. I became, as usual, more and more engaged and a few days later I had attracted additional crows by laying out tallow so I could continue working with their facial expressions. I had intended it to become a study in grey, but could not resist adding a birch leaf with warmer tones, after having collected a couple of still leafed branches as reference material.

Grey Autumn Colours 2007
Hooded Crows
Oil 81 x 100 cm

149

Study of Chaffinch 2006
Oil 22 x 27 cm

A mong the dry herbaceous perennial plants that holds their stems upright through the winter the Carline Thistle is my favourite. It favours dry soil rich in lime. It usually grows but this season I noticed that they had become quite tall, and their dried yellowish corollas did set off against the grey-coloured snow. On the painting are also dry Chicory and Greater Knapweed as well as a selection of different grasses that I brought back to the studio. The Grey Partridge is common on southern Gotland but, just like the Carline Thistle, does their presence becomes really obvious when the ground gets snow-covered. Few birds seem to stretch their wings as often as the partridges; it is as if they constantly need to ensure that all the primaries are in good shape. They do not habitually fly, but when a predator attacks they explode into flight. The Goshawk and the Red Fox are the most obvious threats to the adult birds.

Winter Weeds 2006
Grey Partridges
Oil 60 x 80 cm

In a group of birds, there is often one which is the centre, or is the one the onlooker communicates with. The other individuals are important for the wholeness, and are there to support the eye's search towards the "centre". I usually do not decide on this, where the centre is or which bird should be dominant, from the beginning. The space, which I wish to relate to, gradually grows into the picture.

Picture 1

I imagined an open space in front of the small embankment of snow-covered tufts of grass against which the birds would huddle. The birds would enter from different directions in order to build up the space, where the uncovered tufts of grass would have a double function; as a windbreaker and to dissolve their silhouettes from a raptor's eye. The bird on the right in the row of four became the main subject and what was between this bird and the next one became the centre of the space. It felt completely natural when I started to paint these.

Picture 2

The idea of the bird, which I planned to come in from the left, was that it should enforce the feeling of the birds gathering together and that the tracks in the snow would show that they had entered from different directions. As I painted this bird, the main figure became more communicative with the incoming one, the energy was moved to a level above the snow cover and the other tracks in the snow were deprived of their intrinsic value. In cases like this when I realise that the picture is not in harmony, I have to use "trial and error" to find where the fault lies.

Picture 3

When I covered the left bird with a white sheet of paper, I could meet the look of my main bird again, and the plane in front of the birds became visible once more. That is why I removed the bird that originally was intended to mark the movement towards the centre. Instead it became the tracks which carried this movement in a more interesting way. When we catch the main figure's face we can interpret the tracks peripherally, then we continue to the other birds and interpret them before going back to the centre and, in this way, the onlooker's eye gathers this "to and fro" motion together and creates a movement. In picture two it is always the birds at the far end which attract us when we try to fixate on the bird in the middle and the onlooker in that way draws the group apart. The bird that enters from the right and focuses on a blade of grass has an important function in that it holds on to our main figure from the right and counterbalances the scene so that the centre remains where it is. When I covered that bird with my paper the picture became too heavy on the left side, it capsized. If the bird would have looked towards us it would pull the picture apart.

Winter Tracks 2005
Grey Patridges
Oil 81 x 100 cm

153

I have always carried with me the interest for birds and field identification since I started to draw. The free painting and the illustrations for field guides and identification papers have always been branches on the same tree. Basically, it is about researching visually, interpreting and then conveying the impressions.

Flying Black-throated Loon and Common Loon
Illustration for *Lommar* (Loons)
Watercolour 17 x 22 cm

First two volumes of *Fåglar i naturen*

It has been important for me to convey life and movement within the tight framework of ornithological illustration, to create a feeling of the birds' presence. I was told early on that due to pedagogical reasons it was better to reproduce the birds in the same angle and pose to facilitate comparisons. I could never follow that advice as I wanted rather to paint the birds as large as possible to be able to show details that I thought were interesting and attractive and to give my plates life. I thus composed the birds as large as possible and many of them twist and turn in order to fit onto the sheet. I may have lost something by doing that, but the work became more fun and developing. It is especially visible in the plates I did in the early seventies. For the last two volumes in my series of *European Birds,* which were aimed more at geographical regions, I could work to a greater extent with the nature in the background which I perceived as more exciting.

On and off I spent the larger part of the 80s merging the five volumes into one, *The Birds of Europe with North Africa and the Middle East* (1992). The field identification of birds was an area that developed quickly during the 70s and 80s and new, authoritative articles were published one after the other. In *Birds of Sea and Coast*, which was published in 1978, I could get away with writing "the juvenile plumages of the three species of skuas (jaegers)are difficult to distinguish from each other", but by the late 80s each species had to be meticulously described. The new plates became stricter in order to present all new information.

The most difficult challenges in field identification had a strong attraction for me and, parallel with work on the field guide in the 80s, I submerged myself into small sandpipers of the genus *Calidris* 1981-1984, Loons 1984-1992 and Jaegers 1985-1990 which resulted in different publications. In the 90s it was large gulls, a project that still continues.

Eurasian Siskin and European Greenfinch 1974
Illustration for *Birds of Wood, Park and Garden* 1978
Watercolour 31 x 20 cm

Temminck´s Stint, Little Stint and Sanderling 1974–75
Illustration for *Birds of Sea and Coast* 1978
Watercolour and gouache 34 x 24 cm

Juvenile Pomarine Jaeger, Parasitic Jaeger and Long-tailed Jaeger
Illustration for *Birds of Europe with North Africa and the Middle East* 1992
Watercolour and gouache 36 x 24 cm

Rustic Bunting and Little Bunting
Illustration for *Birds of Mountain Regions* 1979
Watercolour and gouache 34 x 24 cm

Lesser Spotted Woodpecker and
Three-toed Woodpecker
Illustration for *Birds of Europe* 1992
Watercolour and gouache 30 x 24 cm

This plate was originally done for *Birds of Mountain Regions* (1978), but was repainted for the combined volume. A female Lesser Spotted Woodpecker was added and the whole background was painted in, inspired after having spent the whole of April 1986 in Lapland.

As a young bird-watcher with Peterson's *Birds of Britain and Europe* in my hand I travelled in my dreams to the countries around the Meditteranean where I imagined myself seeing all the new species of birds of prey, warblers and wheatears. The first real experience of the Mediterreanean bird fauna was in May 1975 when I went to Greece with some birding friends. The strongest memories are from the Arava valley north of Alexandropolis where all my expectations of "Arcadia" came through. Golden Orioles, Bee-eaters, Woodchat Shrike, Masked Shrikes, Olivaceous Warbler, everything just appeared in front of our eyes, and above us; along the ridge an Imperial Eagle was gliding by and Booted Eagles displayed over the oak covered hills. During the latter half of the 70s I made many trips for

my last volume *Birds of the Mediterrenean and the Alps* (1980) and fell in love with many places. Two trips to Turkey, both in 1978, created strong memories, especially the adventurous hikes into the Tauros mountain in search of high alpine species. On the mountain of Ala Dag above 10 500 feet two Lammergiers came in and passed less than 10 metres above me. I could look into their strange prehistoric eyes and hear the wind whine in their tinplate-like wingfeathers.

After having completed the five volumes I spent the spring of 1980 in Spain, where I tried to find myself as a painter.

Lammergeier Coming in for the Night
Uluborlu, Turkey September 1978
Watercolour 36 x 25 cm

Bonelli´s Eagles
Sierra de Rondo, Spain 23.8.1980
Watercolour 46 x 31 cm

Egyptian Vulture and Lammergeier 1978–79
Illustration for *Birds of the Mediterranean Region* 1981
Watercolour and gouache 34 x 24 cm

Red-rumped Wheatear, Red-tailed Wheatear and White-crowned Wheatear
Illustration for *Birds of Europe* 1992
Watercolour and gouache 35 x 26 cm

Cyprus Pied Wheatear, Mourning Wheatear and Hooded Wheatear
Illustration for *Birds of Europe* 1992
Watercolour and gouache 35 x 26 cm

Study of Desert Wheatear
Rivet 15.10.2000
Watercolour and pencil 32 x 50 cm

inner secondaries fading out
like desert wheater

mellowish blackish eye
translating.
marginal coverts slight sandy

primary tips
hard to discern

pd white above
lores. broad off white
or rather dirty
light sage-white
supercilium
above ear coverts,
though not
an obvious supere.
at distance

lull allberg

Lanius excubitor
pallidirostris

Anniv/Soudane 31.8.95

Study of Southern Grey Shrike
Hamra 31.8.1995
Watercolour and pencil 32 x 25 cm

If any birds pose challenges to portray, it is the common and unobtrusive species. The Willow Warbler, the commonest bird in Sweden, or young Dunlins for example. In the encounters they are always experienced as typical, yet always individual. To sum up their variation in one individual bird is pointless; it is rather about choosing a bird that feels typical. Equipped with a wealth of sketches and a plethora of photographs I decided once and for all to paint the definite Willow Warbler. But as soon as I tried to delineate it, to define its characters, it gradually died off. The experience of movement, the tail that is raised or lowered, the mild, petite face which turns in the search for insects, the small feet which alternatively slide down along a branch or grip a twig firmly; all of this which is the Willow Warbler hardens on paper. Killian Mullarney, a friend and colleague, worked during the nineties with plates for the *Collins Bird Guide*. He once confided to me that, after having studied my Radde's Warbler, he promised himself that he would do it better, with his fresh experiences and sketches of this vagrant from eastern Siberia. His resulting painting is wonderful, but he felt, just like me, that there was a discrepancy between what he knew and what the result was; something seems to be lost regardless of how much one labours. My warblers in *Birds of Europe* involved many hours of preparations and hours of detailed work. When I look at the results afterwards I immediately realise the discrepancies; the belly silhouette should be a bit tighter, the angle of the neck more distinct, the lore should be enforced etc. But this is all probably due to the want of seeing it from different angles during a short period of time, i.e. that which constitutes the field experience.

Sketchbook 2006
Studies of Willow Warbler
Blyerts 32 x 50 cm

Willow Warbler, Chiffchaff, Radde´s Warbler and Dusky Warbler
Illustrations for *Birds of Europe* 1992
Watercolour and gouache 35 cm x 26 cm

Loons, comprising only five species in the world, became one of my great interests in the eighties. The two large species, Great Northern and White-billed, were rare but regular on migration and seldom encountered in winter. They were more regular in Norway and I cooperated with Toralf Tysse there in a project which involved identifying them in the field. The project started to develop when I became interested in their plumage changes and turned out to be more complicated than expected. They are often far out at sea and light conditions are unfavourable. I therefore visited many museums to sort out their moult patterns, but most collections were not representative of what we encountered in the field. The most exciting discovery was the second summer plumage of the Yellow-billed Loon which had never been described before in literature. During a trip to northern Norway in the autumn of 1986, I had some incompara-

ble experiences with Yellow-billed Loons. It seems that the species' eyesight is rather poor outside of water and if one sits they appear to be attracted closer to investigate the figure on the shore. A total of nine birds came so close on one quiet night that I could see their red irises and the pattern of each individual feather. The large painting to the right was overambitious in its attempt to show the character of each individual feather. Afterwards I felt that something in the general impression of the bird became lost in the purpose of our book; to identify these species in the field. I made the new plate so it could be used for both the book Lommar (Loons) and the merged version of my field guides. This resulted in that both species got a new spread in the latter, which perhaps was not really motivated. Both books were published in 1992.

Neckpatterns of swimming Loons
Illustration for *Lommar (Loons)* 1992
Watercolour 15 x 22 cm

Yellow-billed Loon
Illustration for *Birds of Europe* 1992
Watercolour and gouache 36 x 24 cm

Yellow-billed Loon
Illustration for *Lommar (Loons)* 1992
Watercolour and gouache 38 x 24 cm

I think it all began with a simple question from the late Peter Grant (1943 –1990), he wanted my opinion about the form of Herring Gull named "heuglini" that bred on the tundra from the Kola peninsula and eastwards. He was working with the second edition of his *Gulls, a Guide to Identification* (1986) that was a milestone when published in 1982. He asked about my opinion regarding that large dark-backed gulls that most likely would turn up in the Baltic. I gave him some answers without really knowing anything, and with this came the frustration – we have a gull breeding close to Scandinavia that we basically do not know anything about. Already in the late 1900-hundreds this subspecies was a hot topic among taxonomists and much was written during the first decades of the twentieth century, but due to the closed Soviet Union the "case" was more or less forgotten. I kept my eyes open but not until 1994, when I participated on an expedition to arctic Russia, was I able to observe these birds in the field. It would turn out to be the start of a project that ever since has taken me to many places and museums around the northern hemisphere in order to get a better understanding of their relationship and characteristics. No other family of birds do I feel more familiar with then some of these large gulls. A lot of the work is done in museum collections which statistic results gives me a

tool to interpret what I observe in the field. I have in my field studies been trying to capture the overall look as well as detailed information regarding individual feathers and moult. My collection consists of hundreds of gull-portraits. Nowadays I regard the collection itself as a kind of artwork. The individual studies have the information collected at the time, but the combined effort becomes in a way an artistic representation of the endless variation in nature – as well as an expression of my own obsession. They are all individual birds that carry a piece of a great puzzle, the one of Evolution. With great excitement have I several times portrayed what appeared to be the missing link, just to understand that it only gave me new questions. The feedback is always partly aestethic, whether it is the softness of a grey mantle, the intriguing pattern of a young gull's tail or the beauty of the scientific connections I could sense. I never thought that I would find statistics aesthetically interesting, but it is. The knowledge of *heuglini* and other gulls is so much greater today, but we still do not have the full picture of how the various forms of gulls have evolved and how they relate to each other. I have since the mid 90s been able to identify a few *heuglini's* on southern Gotland; the above bird was relocated on a field just outside my studio.

Heuglin´s Gull *Larus (fuscus) heuglini*
Faludden 27.5.2002, 2.30–3 pm and Sindarve, 3.30–5.10 pm
Watercolour 42 x 56 cm

170

Secondaries in moult
P10 still growing, P9 almost full
length.

Primary coverts with some moult
Dark area on primaries darker
than typical glaucous winged.

Greater coverts also
in moult

P10 still growing

(Western)/glaucous winged gull
4K 10/11·04
Greenlake, Seattle

I adult with yellow bill

Primaries very black   white tertials

California gull Green Park, Seattle 10.11.04
Amount of dark on head variable
often white eyeing above eyes

Elongated posture

Very much like Mew gull. Eye colour diagnostic
but more strongly obvious yellow

Glaucous-winged Gull
Greenlake, Seattle 10.11.2004
Watercolour 25 x 32 cm

California Gull
Greenlake, Seattle 10.11.2004
Watercolour 25 x 32 cm

*On the Refuse tip in Bahrain Febrary 1996
with a captured gull of the form "heuglini".*

The Puzzle of Gull Evolution 1996–2006
56 pages from sketchbooks 25 x 32 cm
Pencil and watercolour 125 x 510 cm

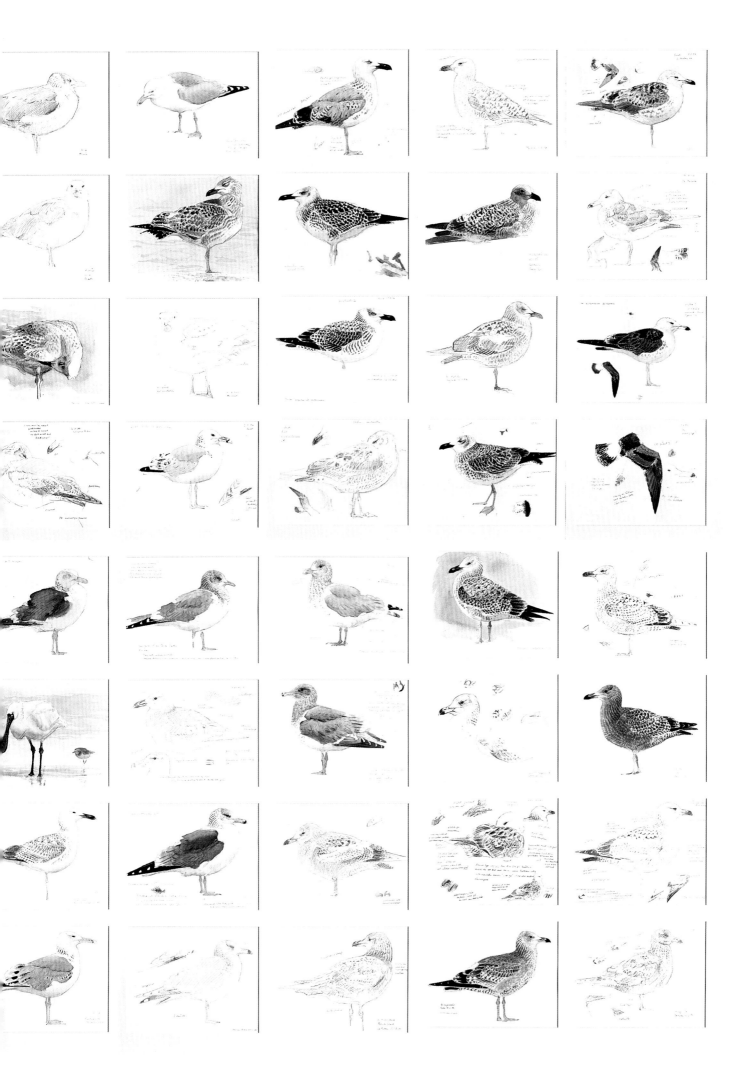

173

I am currently working on a project where I try to fuse my ornithological interest with my philosophy to paint what I see. It is actually three projects, one about ducks, geese and swans, the second is waders and the last will deal with gulls and possibly terns. The goal is to make at least one field sketch of all representatives found in the Holarctic of these three families. The springboard is my acquired experiences from working with field guides. A compressed illustration for a field guide, produced by the drawing board in the studio, can only tell part of the truth. Images of birds painted directly in the field can sometimes bring another dimension of reality, the visual reality, the one that is experienced in real time. I often felt that something precious is lost when a field sketch is transformed into a field guide illustration. These three projects which are expected to result in three books are envisaged to use these experiences as the starting point. I wish to convey an experience as much as depict an appearance. There are several examples of these types of pictures under the heading Sketchbooks. Although I have been working with it, unconsciously, for most of my life there are still birds to paint in different light and plumages, or rather to experience through the use of paper, watercolour and brush. I feel privileged to be able to do just that.

Juvenile female Eider
Rivet 30.9.2006
Watercolour 32 x 50 cm

Ringed Plover
Aurriv, Gotland 6.4.2006
Watercolour (detail)

'kuich'
trädkrypt, smärtigt

Semipalmated Plover
Bolivar flats, Texas 17.4.2006
Watercolour and pencil 32 x 25 cm

1

2

3

4

1 *Against all Winds*
   Great Black-backed Gulls
   61 x 87 cm 2002
   Edition 1–310/310
   HC 1–30/30

2 *Eiderpair*
   44 x 57 cm 2002
   Edition 1–250/250
   HC 1–25/25

3 *Observation*
   Common Gull
   42 x 60 cm 2003
   Edition 1–360/360
   HC 1–35/35

4 *Wintermorning* Magpies
   60 x 43 cm 2003
   Edition 1–360/360
   HC 1–35/35

5

6

7

8

9

5 *The Baltic Sea* Eiders
   59 x 91 cm 2003
   Edition 1–360/360
   HC 1–40/40

6 *Female Eiders*
   41 x 46 cm 2003
   The same print as *The Baltic Sea*
   but part of the edition is torned
   down to a smaller format

7 *Towards North* Eiders
   17 x 20 cm 2003
   Edition 1–360/360
   HC 1–40/40

8 *Short-eared Owl*
   29 x 24 cm 2003
   Edition 1–360/360
   HC 1–40/40

9 *Silent Move* Curlew
   42 x 50 cm 2003
   Edition 1–360/360
   HC 1–40/40

10 *Coastal Meadow*
   Oystercatcher chicks
   37 x 51 cm 2003
   Edition 1–360/360
   HC 1–35/35

10

11

13

12

14

11 *By the Stone* Ringed Plover
    30 x 41 cm 2005
    Edition: 1–360/360
    HC 1–35/35

12 *Small will become Big*
    Oystercatcher with chick
    30 x 41 cm 2005
    Edition: 1–360/360
    HC 1–35/35

13 *Together again* Oystercatchers
    46 x 61 cm 2005
    Edition: 1–310/310
    HC 1–30/30

14 *Longing* Curlew
    40 x 61 cm 2006
    Edition: 1–450/450
    HC 1–45/45

15 *Enclosed* Avocets
    46 x 61 cm 2006
    Edition: 1–360/360
    HC 1–35/35

15

18

16

19

17

16   *In Grey Shimmer* Caspian Terns
     30 x 45 cm 2008
     Edition: 1–310/310
     HC 1–30/30

17   *A Full House*
     Lapwing with chicks
     32 x 45 cm 2008
     Edition: 1–310/310
     HC 1–30/30

18   *Evening Curlews*
     56 x 87 cm 2008
     Edition: 1–310/310
     HC 1–30/30

19   *Première* Arctic Terns
     41 x 61 cm 2008
     Edition: 1–310/310
     HC 1–30/30

1952
Born in Stockholm. Parents are May Jonsson (1926–2004) and Sven Jonsson (1913–1987).

1957
The family starts to spend their summer vacations on the Island of Gotland in the Baltic Sea. He starts to explore the unique nature and birdlife of the island that be-comes his major source of inspiration. His interest in drawing birds is documented as of April that year.

1965
Becomes a member of a bird club, Södertörns Fältbiologer. His talent to paint and draw birds develops during his teens and he starts to keep a diary with notes and sketches.

1968
Jonsson has his first exhibition at the Natural History Museum in Stockholm, at age fifteen.

1969
Travels alone to the Faeroe Islands and during five weeks he explores the islands and paints and writes about its birdlife.

1971
Jonsson graduates from Gubbängens Gymnasium and together with his brother and two friends he travels to Africa in a Volkswagenbus. They cross the Sahara and the journey ends in Cameroon three months later. Participates in an art exhibition in Budapest in conjunction with an international sporting exhibition.

1972
Jonsson applies to the Royal Academy of Art but is not accepted. He documents his ability to draw and paint birds in several exhibitions, as well as through articles in various ornithological magazines. In the exhibition *Birds – Wings – Flight* in Stockholm he exhibits with some well-known Wildlife artists in Sweden. Travels to Istanbul in September to study raptors that migrate over the Bosporus Strait.

1973
Travels to northern Scandinavia in June, to England in September and to southern Spain in December. Supports himself as an artist and exhibits in Visby during the summer and also participates in several group exhibitions. At age twenty-one he is asked to develop a series of new field guides on European birds based on habitats. He presents his ideas in late autumn and gets the commission to produce five volumes over the coming years, a series of books that will be published in seven languages. This major commission takes most of his time during the 70s and will involve him again in the 80s when he will work on a combined version of the five volumes. He describes the work with the field guides as his academy, having to develop both technical skill and strict working discipline. Participates in an exhibition at Galleri Z, near Örebro in November, a gallery where he regularly will exhibit.

1974
Begins work on the two first volumes of *Fåglar i Naturen*. Travels to research for the books to Eastern Europe in May and to England and Ireland in September. Participates in an exhibition at Kalmar konstmuseum with the foremost representatives of Swedish wildlife artists.

1975
Moves to a flat in central Stockholm in January and in October he buys a stone house on southern Gotland. The house will become his home and working studio for the future, and an important place for his development as an artist. It is close to the shore, dominated by coastal meadows grazed by sheep and geese. Participates in several group exhibitions of which *Animals in Art* in Toronto, Canada is the most important. The coming years are dominated by work for the field guides including several research trips abroad, where he also makes many international contacts. He travels to Greece and to northern Finland and Norway.

1976
The first two volumes of *Fåglar i Naturen* are published in Sweden. Appears on Swedish television where he is interviewed and demonstrates his way of painting birds. In July he travels to Iceland.

1977
Travels to Morocco in March, to Spain with his brother in May, and in August to Greece to research birds for the last volume of his fieldguides covering Mediterranean birds. Prints his first lithograph.

1978
Travels to Morocco again in March and makes two major trips to Turkey, one in May and one in September. The first three volumes of his guides is published in several European countries, in England by Penguin Nature Guides, for which he creates the logo. Makes a long promotion and signing tour around England and Scotland in June.

1979
His first major solo show on Gotland opens in Visby in the autumn, organized by the Art Society of Gotland. Travels to Mallorca in August.

1980
Birds of the Mediterranean and the Alps is published in Sweden in the spring. Relieved by the completion of the book series he spends time in Andalusia to paint. Experiments with both watercolour and oil.

1981
Travels to Greece i february and again with some friends in April. During the summer he spends time painting outdoors and he begins to work on the book *Bird Island*, in which he follows the life of a small sandbar in his local bay. Combines his technical skills acquired from working with the bird books with a more vivid and fluid watercolour technique. His watercolours of birds done in the field, develop rapidly into a more personal style. Exhibits at Galleri Händer in Stockholm. Travels to the Americas for the first time, invited to study and work on an article about identification of stints (smaller sandpipers). Meets Arthur Singer and Don Eckelberry. Spends two months in Peru in December and January of 1982.

1982
In the summer he exhibits with an artist friend at a gallery in southern Sweden. In

September, and from this year on, Jonsson participates in the yearly exhibition *Birds in Art* at the Leigh Yawkey Woodson Art Museum (LYWAM) in Wausau, Wisconsin. He will travel almost every year to the U.S. and participate in various exhibitions and events.

1983

The book *Ön, bilder från en sandrevel* is released in Sweden, a book that in words and paintings describes the vibrant but fragile life on a small shoal of sand throughout a short summer. Two major shows follow, where most of the work from the previous two years of extensive painting are exhibited, one at the Naturhistoriska riksmuseet (the National Museum of Natural History) a return after fifteen years. Travels for the first time to the Soviet Union where he visits central Siberia and Kazakhstan. Visits Eilat in southern Israel in November to study birds.

1984

Spends most of the spring in the U.S. where he follows the birds northward from Florida to Alaska, birding 15 different states. Holds a workshop on painting birds in the field in Massachusetts. On the shores of the Bering Strait he watches the sandhill cranes migrate to Russia and he longs to visit arctic Russia. The article about stints is published in *American Birds* and in *British Birds*. *Bird Island, pictures from a shoal of sand* is published in England and he also exhibits at the Tryon Gallery in London.

1985

Marries Ragnhild Erlandsson in February and travels to the Seychelles. Martin their first child is born in June. Visits the westcost of U.S. in September.

1986

The small family spends the whole of April in swedish Lapland. In the autumn travels for two and a half month along the westcoast of U.S. from Seattle to San Diego. Lars paints birds and especially studies the loons. A large painting of Seaotters is compleated on site in California and i exhibited the following year at the exhibition Wildlife in Art at the LYWAM in 1987.

1987

Viktor, their second son is born in April. Exhibits again at the Tryon Gallery in London in October, which is a great success. Afterwards he visits the Scilly Islands. His father dies.

1988

Rebecka is born in August. Receives the Master Wildlife Artist award from the Leigh Yawkey Woodson Art Museum in September, so far the youngest artist to be acknowledged by the museum. During a visit at the Trondheimsfjord in Norway, where he studies Yellow-billed Loons, he brakes his leg. The time in convalescence is

spent planning how to combine the five volumes of birdguides into one. His work with the combined field guide goes into a more intensive period. It will include the birds from the Middle East. He visits Israel in 1988, 1989 and 1990. On Gotland the children are growing and the need for a separate studio results in the acquisition of a nearby barn which he turns into a studio.

1990

With the publication of *En dag i maj* (*A Day in May*) Jonsson continues to describe the birds and nature of southern Gotland from a personal perspective. The book describes the impressions from one single day, the 18th of May 1989, from dawn to dusk.

1991

In June he travels with a group of international birdwatchers to arctic Siberia, a place that he had longed to visit ever since childhood. The dream bird, spoon-billed sandpiper, was found and painted close to Providenya on the Chukotska Peninsula. The interest for this part of the world will bring him back to northern Russia several times in the 90s.

1992

The Birds of Europe with North Africa and the Middle East is published in three languages and becomes a great success. At the same time, the work with Loons that has been underway for several years is also published under the title *Lommar*. He travels to Japan for the first time and continues on to the U.S. After the completion and publication of *Birds of Europe* his painting again comes into focus and especially the oil-painting enters a new phase. It will result in several larger exhibitions in the following years. He exhibits in Paris at the Centre Culturel Suedois and at Galerie Rolf Wahl, as well as the art museum in Uttersberg, Sweden.

1993

Visits the Varanger Peninsula in northeast Norway in May, in order to prepare for a major expedition to arctic Siberia. One-man shows at Härnösands Konsthall and Karlskoga Konsthall.

1994

Visits Extremadura, Spain in March to participate in a project organized by Artist for Nature Foundation (ANF). In May opens an exhibition at Kalmar Konstmuseum where he is shown together with works by Bruno Liljefors (1860–1939). The major event this year, however, is the expedition to arctic Siberia organized by the Swedish Polar Research Institute. It is a Russian-Swedish expedition which uses the vessel Academic Federov and helicopters to cover many places along the arctic coast of Russia. During the two months spent with the expedition, he paints and writes down his experiences with a wide range of arctic wildlife, including

encounters with polar bears. In September, he is engaged by the Massachusetts Audubon Society to paint for their centennial book, *The Nature of Massachusetts* that will be published in 1996. Matilda, their second daughter and fourth children is born in December.

1995

The experiences from the arctic expedition are presented in a show with two other artists at the National Museum of Natural History in Stockholm. Spends most of May in Massachusetts. In summer, a major exhibition at the Gotland Art Museum based on his Kalmar show. Travels to Bahrain in November to study gulls. The increasing interest for the evolution and identification of large gulls will occupy Jonsson in the second half of the 90´s and bring him to various places in Asia. During 1995–97 a documentary is done about Lars and the film is shown on national television in 1998.

1996

Back to Bahrain in February. In May travels to Yakutia and the river Ob to watch Siberian White Cranes as well as gulls. Exhibition at Höganäs Museum in Sweden. Publication of *The Nature of Massachusetts* brings him to the U.S. and an exhibition in Canton, Massachusetts.

1997

Exhibits again together with works of Bruno Liljefors at the Örebro Castle. Travels to Austria and Hungary in juky to study gulls. Participates for the first time in *Western Vision*, at the National Museum of Wildlife Art in Jackson Hole, Wyoming, a show and place that he returns to annually. In November he again joins ANF for a project in Bandawgard in central India to help save the tigers. It will result in a book and an exhibition at the Burrel Collection in Glasgow in 2000.

1998

The Gull research takes him to the steppes around Omsk and to Krasnoyarsk in central Siberia.

1999

Exhibition in Brussels. In February travels to Japan to study gulls and other birds. Also exhibits at the Uttersberg Art Museum. In November to Taiwan invited to an international wildlife art exhibition in Taipei.

2000

A new book is published *Dagrar* (*Daylight reflections*). It is the third book that, with Jonsson´s own artwork and excerpts from his diaries, describes the local birdlife and landscape.

A portfolio with 12 lithographs and a specially bound edition of the book is published. Exhibit at Österbybruk, Sweden in the house where Bruno Liljefors had lived and worked, organized

by the Bruno Liljefors Foundation. Travels to Niagara Falls in December as keynote speaker at a gull conference.

2002
Receives an honorary doctorate from Uppsala University. In October a retrospective exhibiti-on opens at the Prins Eugens Waldemarsudde, a part of the National Museum of Art, in Stockholm. The book and catalogue *Fåglar och Ljus (Birds and Light)* is published in conjunction with the opening, and will be released in English and French. The exhibition turns out to be among the ten most visited in the history of the Museum. Jonsson makes several appearances on national TV.

2003
His exhibition in Stockholm travels to Ronneby Konsthall in the beginning of the year. Jonsson travels to Hokkaido in Japan to spend some time painting birds prior to joining a cruise ship that travels along the Kurile Islands to Kamchatka and the islands in the Bering Strait. In Novem-ber again joins ANF for a project in Northern Peru and Ecuador, where the artists portray the unique nature and birdlife of the Tumbes region.

2004
His mother dies. Travels with Ragnhild to India in March. On Gotland, the Museum Lars

Jonsson opens at the old vicarage of Vamlingbo Parish. The book *Treasures of a Forgotten Forest* is published in conjunction with an art exhibition at the British Birdwatching Fair and later at the Wildlife Art Gallery in Lavenham. Travels in November to Washington State and New Mexico to paint birds of prey.

2005
In June exhibits at the Gerald Peters Gallery in Santa Fe, the exhibition *From Wild Skies* features paintings of birds of prey by Jonsson, Tony Angel and Thomas Quinn. Travels with the whole family to Botswana and South Africa over Christmas and the New Year, where for the first time they together have the opportunity to watch the large African mammals.

2006
Teaches a workshop in Texas in April on how to paint birds in the field, and also studies American waders. In summer he exhibits at Borstahusens Konsthall, Landskrona. Travels to Washington, D.C. to prepare for a show in 2007 at the newly built Swedish embassy. He spent some time on the Delmarva peninsula painting waterfowl.

2007
In March the exhibition *Wings over Northern Shores* opens at Anna Lind Hall, House of

Sweden in Washington, D.C. Returns to the U.S. in September and paints waders in Massachusetts.

2008
The exhibition *Wo Erde und Himmel sich berühren/ Where Heaven and Earth Touch* opens in July at the Landesmuseum für Natur und Mensch, Oldenburg and in Kastrupsgaardssamlingen, Copenhagen in September. During 2009 it will travel to Vendsyssel Konstmuseum, Hjörring; Deutsches Jagd- und Fischereimuseum, Munich; Heimatmuseum Schloss Adelsheim, Berchtesgaden; Naturhistorische Museum, Vienna, Austria and the LWL-Museum für Naturkunde, Münster, Germany. A catalouge is published in conjunction with the exhibitions in English and German.

MUSEUM LARS JONSSON
The museum is in the main building at the Vamlingbo vicarage on southern Gotland. The buil-ding is from 1779. The galleries show recent and older works by the artist.
www.larsjonsson.se

SOLO EXHIBITIONS

1968
Naturhistoriska Riksmuseet, Stockholm

1970
Biblioteket i Västerhaninge, Stockholm
Biblioteket i Handen, Stockholm
Gubbängens gymnasium, Stockholm
Gröndalsskolan, Nynäshamn

1972
Galleri Hos Oss, Visby
Karolinska sjukhuset,
    Galleri »Gången«, Stockholm

1973
Galleri Z, Odensbacken (Örebro)

1976
Galleri Z, Odensbacken

1977
Galleri Z, Odensbacken

1978
Galleri Z, Odensbacken

1979
Forum (Gotlands Konstförening), Visby

1980
Göran Boström · Lars Jonsson
    Galleri Z, Odensbacken

1981
Galleri Händer, Stockholm
Agneta Engström · Lars Jonsson ·
    Jurgen af Rolén Galleriet, Konst &
        Hantverkshuset, Sanda, Gotland

1982
Gunnar Brusewitz Fårö · Lars Jonsson Sudret
    Galleriet, Konst & Hantverkshuset, Sanda
Lars Jonsson · Jurgen af Rolén
    Galleri W, Simrishamn

1983
Ön, bilder från en sandrevel
    Galleriet, Konst & Hantverkshuset, Sanda
Galleri Astley, Uttersberg
Lars Jonsson · Harald Wiberg
    Galleri Z, Odensbacken
Naturhistoriska Riksmuseet, Stockholm
Galleri Falbygden, Falköping

1984
Bird Island (book release)
    Tryon Gallery, London

1985
Börstorps slott, Mariestad

1986
Galleriet, Konst & Hantverkshuset,
    Sanda Gotland

1987
Bird Reflections
    Tryon & Moorland Gallery, London
Björn Dal · Lars Jonsson · Staffan Ullström
    Galleri Z, Odensbacken

1990
En dag i maj Galleriet, Konst &
    Hantverkshuset, Sanda

1992
Les oiseaux de Lars Jonsson
    Centre Culturel Suédois, Paris
Galerie Rolf Wahl, Paris
Konstmuseet i Uttersberg, Uttersberg
Fåglar i Europa Galleriet, Konst &
    Hantverkshuset, Sanda

1993
Härnösands Konsthall
    (Härnösands Konstförening), Härnösand
Galleri Z, Odensbacken
Karlskoga Konsthall
    (Karlskoga Konstförening), Karlskoga

1994
Grafik och skisser Konstnärshuset, Stockholm
Bruno Liljefors · Lars Jonsson
    Kalmar Konstmuseum, Kalmar

1995
Konstnärer på tundran
    Naturhistoriska Riksmuseet, Stockholm
Gotlands Konstmuseum, Visby
Galleri S, Östersund

1996
Björn von Rosen · Lars Jonsson
    Galleri Kavaletten, Stockholm
Höganäs Museum, Höganäs
The Nature of Massachusetts
    The Massachusetts Audubon Society,
        Canton, MA

1997
Lars Jonsson · Bruno Liljefors
    Örebro Slott, Örebro
Galleriet, Konst & Hantverkshuset, Sanda

1998
Orangeriet, Linnéträdgården
    (Konstsommar i Uppsala), Uppsala
Galleri Z, Odensbacken

1999
Galerie de Pierpont (Golf de Pierpont), Bryssel
Folkets hus konsthall (Alvesta Allmänna
    Konstförening), Alvesta
Dagrar (Millennium Portfolio), Konstmuseet
    Galleri Astley, Uttersberg

2000
Dagrar Österbybruks Herrgård
    (Bruno Liljeforsstiftelsen), Österbybruk

2001
Brunnsta värdshus (Metallförbundet Volvo),
    Eskilstuna, later to Eskilstuna

2002
Fåglar och Ljus
    Prins Eugens Waldemarsudde, Stockholm

2003
Fåglar och Ljus Kulturcentrum (Ronneby
    Kulturförening), Ronneby
Galleri GL, Stockholm

2004
Grafioteket, Stockholm
Museum Lars Jonsson (2004–2008)
    Vamlingbo Prästgård, Gotland

2005
From Wild Skies (Tony Angel · Lars Jonsson ·
    Thomas Quinn) Gerald Peters Gallery,
        Santa Fe, NM

2006
Robert Bateman · Lars Jonsson · Kent Ullberg
    Quinta Manzatlan, McAllen, Texas
Pumphusets Konsthall
    (Borstahusens konstförening), Landskrona
Galleri Bergman
    Alsters herrgård, Karlstad
Galleri Roger, Linköping

2007
Wings over Northern Shores, Anna Lind Hall
House of Sweden, Washington D.C.
Galleri Z, Odensbacken

2008
Where Earth and Heaven Touch
Landesmuseum für Natur und Mensch,
Oldenburg
Travelling exhibition 2008-2009:
Kastrupgaardssamlingen, Copenhagen
Vendsyssel Konstmuseum, Hjörring
Deutsches Jagd- und Fischereimuseum,
Munich
Heimatmuseum Schloss Adelsheim,
Berchtesgaden
Naturhistorische Museum, Vienna
LWL-Museum für Naturkunde, Münster
Lars Bohman Gallery, Stockholm

GROUP EXHIBITIONS

1971
Liljewalchs vårsalong Liljewalchs Konsthall,
Stockholm
Sommarutställning
(Gotlands bildningsförbund)
Biblioteket, Burgsvik, Gotland
Katthamra Gård, Katthamra, Gotland
Sudersands Badrestaurang, Fårö, Gotland
Exp. mondiale de la chasse - exposition
artistique, Budapest

1972
Unga tecknare Nationalmuseet, Stockholm
Fåglar – Vingar – Flykt
Sveagalleriet, Stockholm
Leva med naturen
Naturhistoriska Riksmuseet, Stockholm
Naturen som motiv Borås Museum, Borås
Naturen som motiv Örebro Läns Museum,
Naturen som motiv Skara Teater, Skara

1974
Naturen som motiv Konsthallen Skellefteå
Allan Andersson · Gunnar Brusewitz · Lars
Jonsson ·Harald Wiberg (Galleri Z),
Fiskingegården Asker, Örebro

1975
Animals in Art Royal Ontario Museum,
Toronto

1976
Djur i natur Kalmar konstmuseum, Kalmar

1979
Jubileumsutställning 1969–1979
Fiskingegården, Asker, Örebro

1980
Gunnar Brusewitz · Lars Jonsson · Harald
Wiberg Galleriet, Konst & Hantverkshuset
Sanda, Gotland
Djur och natur Klippans bibliotek
(Klippans Konstförening), Klippan, Skåne

1982
Birds in Art LYWAM (Leigh Yawkey Woodson
Art Museum) Wausau, WI

1983
Birds in Art Exhibition LYWAM, Wausau, WI
Travelling exhibition:
Explorers Hall, National Geographic
Society, Washington D.C.
Denver Museum of Natural History,
Denver, CO (1984)
Houston Museum of Natural Science,
Houston, TX (1984)

1984
Galleri Z, Odensbacken, Örebro
Birds in Art LYWAM, Wausau, WI
Travelling exhibition:
San Bernadino County Museum,
Redlands, CA
California Academy of Sciences,
San Francisco, CA
University of Alaska Museum,
Fairbanks, AK (1985)
Anchorage Historical and Fine Arts
Museum, Anchorage, AK (1985)
Alaska State Museum, Juneau, AK (1985)
Northern shores Saga gallery
(Saga, Scandinavian Art Ltd), London

1985
Galleri Falbygden, Falköping
Inaugural Exhibition for Society of Wildlife Art
for the Nation (SWAN)
Guildhall Art Gallery, London
Birds in Art 1985 LYWAM, Wausau, WI
Travelling exhibition:
Rochester Museum and Science Center,
Rochester, NY
Missouri Botanical Garden, St. Louis,
MI (1986)
Springfield Science Museum, Springfield,
MA (1986)

1986
Bevingat Konstcentrum, Gävle
Birds in Art 1986 LYWAM, Wausau, WI
Travelling exhibition:
Frye Art Museum, Seattle, WA
Santa Barbara Museum of Natural History,
Santa Barbara, CA (1987)
Bernice Pauahi Bishop Museum,
Honolulu, Hawaii (1987)
Beijing Natural History Museum,
Beijing (1987)

1987
Stockholm Art Fair (Galleri Astley),
Stockholm
Wildlife in Art LYWAM Wausau, WI
Travelling exhibition:
Cumming Nature Center, Rochester, NY
Museum & Science Center, Naples, NY
Lakeview Museum of Arts and Sciences,
Peoria, IL
Huntington Galleries, Huntington, WV
Cincinnati Museum of Natural History,
Cincinnati, OH
The R.W. Norton Art Gallery,
Shreveport, LA (1988)
Cumberland Museum and Science,

Nashville, TN (1988)
Springfield Science Museum, Springfield,
MA (1988)
Anniston Museum of Natural History,
Anniston, AL (1988)
Milwaukee Public Museum, Milwaukee,
WI (1988)
Gibbes Art Gallery, Charleston,
SC (1989)
Grafikutställning Galleriet,
Konst & Hantverkshuset, Sanda, Gotland
Birds in Art 1987 LYWAM, Wausau, WI
Travelling exhibition:
Rochester Museum and Science Center,
Rochester, NY
Natural History Museum of Los Angeles
County, Los Angeles, CA (1988)
Field Museum of Natural History,
Chicago, IL (1988)

1988
Stockholm Art Fair (Galleri Astley), Stockholm
Birds in Art 1988 LYWAM, Wausau, WI
Travelling exhibition:
Missouri Botanical Garden, St.Louis,
MO (1989)
Cincinnati Museum of Natural History,
Cincinnati, OH (1989)
High Desert Museum, Bend, OR (1989)

1989
D´apres Nature La Galerie d´Art Municipale
(Des musées de la Ville de Luxembourg et
le Musée National d´Histoire Naturelle),
Luxemburg
Stockholm Art Fair (Galleri Astley), Stockholm
Jubileumsutställning »Dygnet Runt«
Fiskingegården, Asker, Örebro
Birds in Art 1989 LYWAM, Wausau, WI
Travelling exhibition:
Houston Museum of Natural Science,
Houston, TX
Arnot Art Museum, Elmira,
NY (1990)
Anchorage Museum of History and Art,
Anchorage, AK (1990)
Patrick & Beatrice Haggerty Museum of
Art, Milwaukee, WI (1990)
Grafikutställning Galleri S, Östersund

1990
Rovfåglar (Nationalmuseet, Naturhistoriska
Riksmuseet, Riksutställningar, Uppsala
Universitet), Lövsta herrgård,
Lövstabruk
Stockholm Art Fair (Galleri Astley), Stockholm
Jubileum – Galleriet 10 år Galleriet, Konst &
Hantverkshuset, Sanda, Gotland
Birds in Art 1990 LYWAM, Wausau, WI
Travelling exhibition:
High Desert Museum, Bend, Oregon
Fine Arts Museum of the South,
Mobile, AK (1991)
Rochester Museum and Science Center,
Rochester, NY (1991)
Wendell Gilley Museum, Southwest
Harbor, ME (1991)

1991
Stockholm Art Fair (Galleri Astley), Stockholm
Luft Ängvards salong, Vamlingbo, Gotland
28th Annual Exhibition, Society of Animal
    Artists, Mall Galleries, London
Birds in Art 1991 LYWAM, Wausau, WI
Travelling exhibition:
    American Museum of Natural History.
        New York City, New York
    Ward Museum of Wildfowl Art,
        Salisbury, MA (1992)
    Washington State Historical Society,
        Tacoma, WA (1992)

1992
Stockholm Art Fair (Galleri Astley),Stockholm
Djur och Natur i Konsten Galleri Linné, Sala
Drawn from life Wildlife Art Gallery, Lavenham
Birds in Art 1992 LYWAM, Wausau, WI
Travelling exhibition:
    Buffalo Museum of Science, Buffalo, NY
    Carnegie Museum of Natural History,
        Pittsburgh, PA (1993)
    High Desert Museum, Bend, OR (1993)
Art and the Animal (Society of Animal Artists)
    Roger Tory Peterson Institute of
        Natural History, Jamestown, NY
Travelling exhibition:
    R:W:Norton Art Gallery, Shreveport, LA
    Oklahoma Museum of Natural History,
        Norman, OK
    Oshkosh Public Museum, Oshkosh, WI

1993
Stockholm Art Fair (Galleri Astley), Stockholm
Djur och Natur i Konsten Galleri Linné, Sala
30th Annual Exhibitions, Society of Wildlife
    Artists, Mall Galleries, London
Birds in Art 1993 LYWAM, Wausau, WI
Travelling exhibition:
    New Mexico Museum of Natural History
        and Science, Albaquerque, NM
    Dayton Museum of Natural History,
        Dayton, OH (1994)
    Museum of the Rockies, Bozeman,
        MT (1994)

1994
Djur och Natur i Konsten Galleri Linné, Sala
Birds in Art 1994 LYWAM, Wausau, WI
Travelling exhibition:
    Naturhistoriska Riksmuseet, Stockholm
    Hunter Museum of Art, Chattanooga,
        TN (1995)
Under fågelsträcket Falsterbo Konsthall,
    Falsterbo

1995
Djur och Natur i Konsten Galleri Linné, Sala
The flight of the Cranes ANF in Extremadura,
    Zeist Castle, Zeist
Travelling exhibition:
    Museo de Cirencias-Naturalis, Madrid
    Claustro Garcia-Matos, Caceres
    Centro Cultural Iglesias De San Francisco,
        Trujillo (1996)
    Wildlife Art Gallery, Lavenham (1996)
    LYWAM, Wausau, WI (1997)
Wildlife Art Christie's South Kensington
    (in association with WWF), London,
Birds in Art 1995 LYWAM, Wausau, WI

Travelling exhibition:
    Waterfowl Festival Inc., Easton, ML
    Wendell Gilley Museum, Southwest
        Harbor, ME (1996)
A brush with nature (Wildfowl & Wetlands
    Trust, Slimbridge) Painswick House,
    Gloucestershire

1996
Djur och Natur i Konsten Galleri Linné, Sala
Birds in Art 1996 LYWAM, Wausau, WI
Travelling exhibition:
    Dayton Museum of Natural History,
        Dayton, OH
    James Ford Bell Museum of Natural History,
        MN (1997)
    National Museum of Wildlife Art, Jackson,
        WY (1997)
Samtida konstnärer ser på Liljefors
    Prins Eugens Waldemarsudde, Stockholm

1997
Wonders of Nature – World of Wildlife Art
    (Mondiale Fine Arts) National
        Gallery, Colombo
Wonders of Nature – Hunters in the Wild
    (Mondiale Fine Arts) Holiday Inn Crowne
        Plaza, Dubai
Djur och Natur i Konsten Galleri Linné, Sala
Birds in Art 1997 LYWAM, Wausau, WI
Travelling exhibition:
    Lakeview Museum of Arts and Sciences,
        Peoria, IL (1998)
    Michelson Museum of Art, Marshall,
        TX (1998)

1998
Djur och Natur i Konsten Galleri Linné, Sala
Birds in Art 1998 LYWAM, Wausau, WI
Travelling exhibition:
    Museum of the Southwest, Midland,
        TX (1999)
    Lindsay Wildlife Museum, Walnut Creek,
        CA (1999)
    Delaware Museum of Natural History,
        Wilmington, DE (1999)

1999
Djur och Natur i Konsten Galleri Linné, Sala
Western Visions National Museum of
    Wildlife Art, Jackson Hole, WY
Birds in Art 1999 LYWAM, Wausau, WI
Travelling exhibition:
    Saginaw Art Museum, Saginaw, MI (2000)
    Wendell Gilley Museum, Southwest
        Harbor, ME (2000)
    Michelson Museum of Art, Marshall,
        TX (2000)
Eco Art Exhibition (Taipei Eco Art Association)
    National Museum of History,   Taipei

2000
Wild Tigers of Bandhavgarh (ANF in India)
    Burrell Collection, Glasgow
Travelling exhibition:
    Zeist Castle, Zeist (2001)
    Frankfurt ZOO, Frankfurt (2002)
Djur och Natur i Konsten Galleri Linné, Sala
Wildlife Art for a New Century
    National Museum of Wildlife Art,
        Jackson Hole, WY

Birds in Art 2000 LYWAM Wausau, WI
Western Visions National Museum of
    Wildlife Art, Jackson Hole, WY

2001
Animali nell´Arte Museo Civico di Zoologia,
    Rom
Djur och Natur i Konsten Galleri Linné, Sala
Contemporary Naturalism
    Gerald Peters Gallery, Santa Fe, AZ
Konst på båtarna (Kulturcentralen Ars) Galleri
    Ars Gotlandica, MS Visby,
Birds in Art 2001 LYWAM, Wausau, WI
Travelling exhibition:
    Kennedy Museum of Art, Ohio University,
        Athens, OH
    String Room Gallery, Wells College Aurora,
        NY (2002)
    Linsay Wildlife Museum, Walnut Creek,
        CA (2002)
Western Visions National Museum of
    Wildlife Art, Jackson Hole, WY

2002
Djur och Natur i Konsten Galleri Linné, Sala
Western Visions National Museum of
    Wildlife Art, Jackson Hole, WY
Birds in Art 2002 LYWAM, Wausau, WI
Travelling exhibition:
    Sordoni Art Gallery, Wilkes University
        Wilkes-Barre, PA
    The Wildlife Experience Parker, CO
    Arizona-Sonora Desert Museum
        Tucson, AZ
Nature´s Legacy: Wildlife and Wild Country
    (Sierra Club) Bartfield Gallery,
        New York City, NY
Wildlife and the Artists
    The Wildlife Art Gallery, Lavenham

2003
Birds in Art 2003 LYWAM, Wausau, WI
Travelling exhibition:
    Lindsay Wildlife Museum,
        Walnut Creek, CA
Western Visions National Museum of
    Wildlife Art, Jackson Hole, WY
IV Centuries of Birds Clarke Galleries,
    Stowe, VT

2004
Birds in Art 2004, LYWAM, Wausau, WI
Western Visions National Museum of
    Wildlife Art, Jackson Hole, WY

2005
Birds in Art 2005 LYWAM, Wausau, WI
Western Visions National Museum of
    Wildlife Art, Jackson Hole, WY
Wildlife Art for a New Century II National
    Museum of Wildlife Art, Jackson Hole, WY

2006
Swedish Wildlife Art American Swedish
    Institute, Minneapolis, MN
Birds in Art 2006 LYWAM, Wausau, WI
Western Visions National Museum of
    Wildlife Art, Jackson Hole, WY

190

2007
Natur i konsten Telemarksgalleriet, Kongstad,
    Norge.
Birds in Art 2007 LYWAM, Wausau, WI
Western Visions National Museum of
    Wildlife Art, Jackson Hole, WY

2008
Birds in Art 2008 LYWAM, Wausau, WI
Western Visions National Museum of Wildlife
    Art, Jackson Hole, WY

Fåglar i naturen. Skog, park, trädgård
Wahlström & Widstrand, Stockholm 1976

Fugler i naturen. Skog, park og hage
Cappelen, Oslo 1977

Fugle i naturen. Skov, park og have
Gyldendal, Köpenhamn 1977

Linnut luonnossa. Metsä, puisto ja puutarha
Tammi, Helsingfors 1977

Birds of Wood, Park and Garden
Penguin Books, Harmondsworth 1978

Vögel in Wald, Park und Garten
Franckh, Stuttgart 1977

Vogels in hun eigen omgeving. Tuin en park
B.V. W. J. Thieme & Cie, Zutphen 1977

Os Pássaros. Bosques, parques e jaruins
Círculo de Leitores, Cacém 1977/78

Fåglar i naturen. Hav och kust
Wahlström & Widstrand, Stockholm 1976

Fugler i naturen. Hav og kyst
Cappelen, Oslo 1977

Fugle i naturen. Hav og kyst
Gyldendal, Köpenhamn 1977

Linnut luonnossa. Meri ja rannikko
Tammi, Helsingfors 1977

Birds of Sea and Coast
Penguin Books, Harmondsworth 1978

Die Vögel der Meeresküste
Franckh, Stuttgart 1977

Vogels in hun eigen omgeving. Wad en kust
B.V. W. J. Thieme & Cie, Zutphen 1977

Fåglar i naturen. Sjö, å, träsk och åkermark
Wahlström & Widstrand, Stockholm 1977

Fugler i naturen. Åker, vann og våtmark
Cappelen, Oslo 1978

Fugle i naturen. So og å, mose og mark
Gyldendal, Köpenhamn 1978

Linnut luonnossa. Järvet, joet, suot ja
peltoaukeat Tammi, Helsingfors 1978

Birds of Lake, River, Marsh and Field
Penguin Books, Harmondsworth 1978

Vögel der Fluren und am Wasser
Franckh, Stuttgart 1978

Vogels in hun eigen omgeving. Zoetwater,
moerassen en veld
B.V. W. J. Thieme & Cie, Zutphen 1977

Os Pássaros. Lagos, rios e campos
Círculo de Leitores, Cacém 1977/78

Fåglar i naturen. Fjäll och skogsland
Wahlström & Widstrand, Stockholm 1978

Fugler i naturen. Fjell og barskog
Cappelens, Oslo 1979

Fugle i naturen. Fjeld og fjeldskov
Gyldendal, Köpenhamn 1979

Linnut luonnossa. Tunturit ja havumetsä
Tammi, Helsingfors 1979

Birds of Mountain Regions
Penguin Books, Harmondsworth 1979

Vogels in hun eigen omgeving. Bos, weide en
fjeld
B.V. W. J. Thieme & Cie, Zutphen 1979

Fåglar i naturen. Medelhavsländerna och
Alperna
Wahlström & Widstrand, Stockholm 1980

Fugle i Middelhavslandene og Alperne
Gyldendal, Köpenhamn 1982

Birds of the Mediterranean and Alps
Croom Helm, London 1982

Vogels in hun eigen omgeving. Alpen en
Middellandse Zeegebied
B.V. W. J. Thieme & Cie, Zutphen 1982

Linnut luonnossa. Välimeri ja Alpit
Tammi, Helsingfors 1983

Ön, bilder från en sandrevel
Atlantis, Stockholm 1983

Bird Island, pictures from a shoal of sand
Croom Helm, London 1984

Lintusaaren elämää
Weilin+Göös, Espoo 1988

En dag i maj
Atlantis, Stockholm 1990

Birds of Europe with North Africa and the
Middle East
Christopher Helm, London 1992

Die Vögel Europas und des Mittelmeerraumes
Franckh-Kosmos, Stuttgard 1992

Fåglar i Europa med Nordafrika och
Mellanöstern
Wahlström & Widstrand, Stockholm 1993

Birds of Europe with North Africa and the
Middle East
Princeton University Press, Princeton 1993

Vogels van Europa. Noord-Afrika en het
Midden-Oosten
Tirion, Baarn 1993

Fugler. Europa·Nord-Afrika·Midtosten
Cappelen, Oslo 1994

Fugle i Europa med Nordafrika og Mellemosten,
Gyldendal, Köpenhamn 1994

Euroopan linnut. Eurooppa, Pohjois-Afrikka ja
Lähi-itä,
Tammi, Helsingfors 1994

Les Oiseaux d´Europe, d´Afrique du Nord et du
Moyen-Orient,
Nathan, Paris 1994

Aves de Europa con el Norte de África y el
Próximo Oriente
Ediciones Omega, Barcelona 1994

Ocells d´Europa amb el Nord d´Àfrica i
l´Orient Mitjà
Edicions Omega, Barcelona 1994

Ptaki Europy. I Obszaru `Sròdziemnomorskiego
Muza, Warszawa 1998

192

Euroopa Linnud. Euroopa, Põhja-Aafrika ja
    Lähis-Ida lindude välimääraja
Eesti Entsüklopeediakirjastus, Tallin 2000

Lommar (Jonsson, L. och Tysse, T.)
    Sveriges Ornitologiska Förening,
Stockholm 1992

The Nature of Massachusetts (illustrations,
    text by Leahy, C., Mitchell, J. H., Conuel, T.)
Addison-Wesley, Reading 1996

Dagrar
Wahlström & Widstrand, Stockholm 2000

Fåglar och Ljus
Atlantis, Stockholm 2002

Birds and Light
Christopher Helm, London 2002

La Lumière et les Oiseaux
Nathan, Paris 2002

Wo Erde und Himmel sich berühren
Michael Imhof Verlag, Petersberg 2008

Where Heaven and Earth Touch
Michael Imhof Verlag, Petersburg 2008

Bilder från en nära horisont
Wahlström & Widstrand, Stockholm 2008

Lars Jonsson's Birds
Christopher Helm, London and Princeton
University Press, Princeton 2008

PHOTOGRAPHERS

Page 9, 10—11, 176 Magnus Rietz
Page 14, 16 Anders Hanser
Page 12—13, 15 Karl Melander
Page 137, 183 Gösta Reiland
Other photos by Lars Jonsson